Physical Characteristics of the Whippet

(from The Kennel Club breed standard)

Body: Chest very deep with plenty of heart room. Well filled in front. Brisket deep. Broad, well muscled back, firm, somewhat long, showing graceful arch over the loin but not humped. Ribs well sprung. Loin giving impression of strength and power. Definite tuck up.

Tail: No feathering. Long, tapering, reaching at least to the hock. When in action carried in a delicate curve not higher than the back.

Hindquarters: Strong, broad across thighs, with well developed second thighs. Stifles well bent without exaggeration with hocks well let down. Able to stand naturally over a lot of ground.

Size: Height: dogs: 47–51 cms (18.5–20 ins); bitches: 44–47 cms (17.5–18.5 ins).

Coat: Fine, short, close in texture.

Feet: Oval, well split up between toes, knuckles well arched, pads thick, nails strong.

Colour: Any colour or mixture of colours.

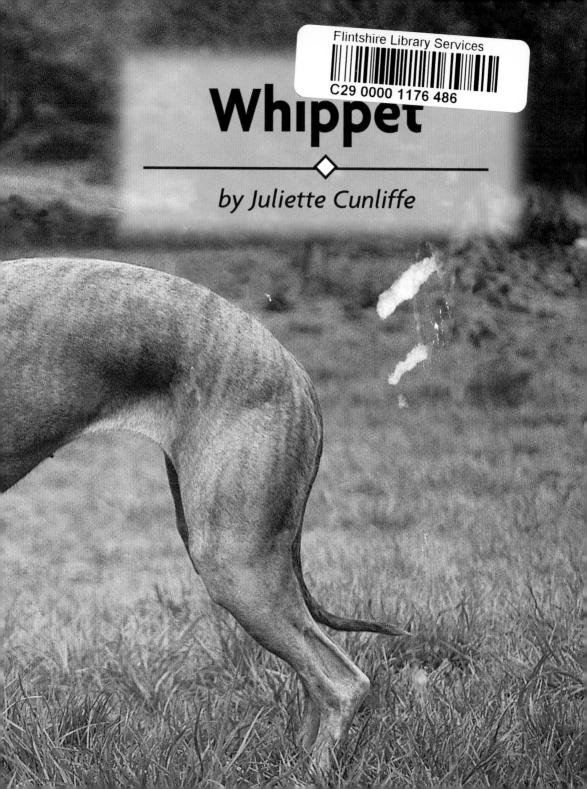

Whippet

◇

by Juliette Cunliffe

Table of Contents

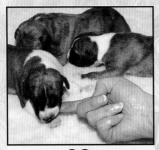

DISTRIBUTED BY:

INTERPET
PUBLISHING

Vincent Lane, Dorking, Surrey RH4 3YX England

ISBN 13: 978 1902389 06 6

PHOTOGRAPHY BY Carol Ann Johnson

with additional photographs by:

Norvia Behling	Bill Jonas
TJ Calhoun	Alice van Kempen
Carolina Biological Supply	Dwight R Kuhn
Juliette Cunliffe	Dr Dennis Kunkel
Tara Darling	Mikki Pet Products
Doskocil	Phototake
Isabelle Francais	Jean Claude Revy
James Hayden-Yoav	Dr Andrew Spielman
James R Hayden, RBP	C James Webb

Illustrations by Renée Low

EARLY SIGHT HOUNDS

The Whippet is one of a number of breeds that falls into the group of dogs classified as sight hounds, often known as gaze hounds. These are hounds that hunt their prey largely by sight; their bodies are lean and powerful, with deep chests and long limbs providing both stamina and speed.

Such hounds are, in general, adapted for finding prey in open country. Once the prey has been located, it can be overtaken by speed and endurance. Because of this special form of hunting, sight hounds have historically been found in regions where there is open countryside, in North Africa, the Arabian countries, Afghanistan, Russia, Ireland and Scotland. The modern Whippet, however, is a more recent member of this highly prized group of dogs and was developed by the miners and mill-hands of the north of England. It was often referred to as 'the poor man's greyhound,' a breed developed for rabbit coursing that later became involved in track racing.

EARLY ANCESTORS

The Asiatic Wolf is most commonly accepted as ancestor of

the sight hounds, for no other wolves are known to have existed in areas where dogs of Greyhound type originated. Although the Whippet is considered a comparatively modern breed, it is worthy of note that the Greeks and Romans used small Greyhounds, these considerably smaller than the breed we know today.

DEVELOPMENT OF THE WHIPPET IN THE NINETEENTH CENTURY

In developing the Whippet, breeders aimed to create a dog that was like a small, fleet Greyhound, but it needed to be hardier than the small Italian Greyhound. Indeed the Whippet needed swiftness and grace as

Illustration of Whippet Ch Enterprise, published in 1900.

Opposite page: An elegant gaze hound, the Whippet has been called 'the poor man's greyhound,' yet anyone who has known the virtues of a Whippet is rich indeed.

9

The Manchester Terrier is believed to have been used in the development of the Whippet, likely contributing its sleek coat and terrier pluck. A Toy Manchester adult and puppy are shown here.

well as pluck and tenacity. With this in mind, several different breeds were involved in its creation. Certainly the Greyhound was used, as was the Italian Greyhound, but there was also Airedale, Bedlington, Manchester, Yorkshire and English Terrier blood mixed in. This terrier blood could be seen in some of the long- or rough-coated dogs found during the early years of the breed's development.

Judicious breeding eventually produced a dog with the staying power of a working terrier combined with the speed and symmetry of the aristocratic sight hounds, its body shape having been gradually refined in harmony with that of the Greyhound. The Whippet we know and love so well today had been born.

The Whippet was once called the 'Hitalian,' alluding to this ancestor, the Italian Greyhound.

BY ANY OTHER NAME
In its early days the Whippet was known by many different names, one of which was 'Snap Dog,' reputed to have arisen because when running along a track or when meeting a strange dog they had a tendency to snap at one another. Another name by which they were known was 'Hitalians,' indicating the breed's Italian Greyhound origin.

It is said that the name

'Whippet' may have been based on the word 'whip,' conveying the breed's sharp character and speed. Having said that, there was a breed called a 'wappit,' described briefly in the early decades of the nineteenth century. Today's Whippet may indeed have some connection with this breed.

KENNEL CLUB RECOGNITION
Whippets were classified as a breed at a show in Darlington in 1876, but the breed was not recognised by The Kennel Club until 1890, the first five Whippets being registered in The Kennel Club's Stud Book the following year. Five was, though, a disappointing number, for it indicated that few owners were interested in actually registering their dogs, considering it a waste of both time and expense. In 1896 the breed was awarded Challenge Certificate (CC) status, leading to what has become today one of the

The Italian Greyhound contributed its rainbow of coat colours and its rose-shaped ears to the Whippet.

most numerically strong breeds on the British show scene. The breed's first champion in Britain was Zuber, who claimed this prestigious title at The Kennel Club Show in October 1896, his first CCs having been awarded at Bath in 1894 and at Crystal Palace in 1895. Ch Zuber was a highly influential sire, as indeed was his son, Ch Enterprise. The first bitch to gain her crown was Ch

The Whippet's arch over its loin and superior ratting ability derive from this dog, the Bedlington Terrier.

DID YOU KNOW?

Quality meat was usually fed to Whippets just for the last few days prior to a race. More usually they ate a basin of broken bread, gravy and pudding, with tea and ale; essentially the same fare as that eaten by the family. Stories of Whippets being fed on bantams' eggs and old sherry are largely figments of the imagination!

11

In the late 1800s, Whippet racing was a sport of the lower classes in England. This stage of the race was called Making Ready. The dogs are thrown into the race, as shown in the photo below, while the rags are used at the finish line. A pistol shot starts the race.

Manorley Model, this at The Kennel Club Show in 1897.

FORMATION OF THE WHIPPET CLUB

In 1899 Britain's Whippet Club was formed, aided to a large extent by that notable dog lady, The Duchess of Newcastle. She was known primarily for her Borzoi and Fox Terriers, but she also exhibited the occasional Whippet and was a dedicated supporter of the breed.

With the formation of a breed club, Kennel Club registrations rose significantly, but understandably during the troubled years of the First World War they declined again, with none registered in 1918.

There were many prominent and influential early kennels, some of which had been set up even before the turn of the century. Again, though, during the Second World War many kennels fell into decline or were completely disbanded. There was a shortage of food, which inevitably had a drastic effect on the breeding and rearing of dogs of all breeds. A few breeders managed to keep their lines going through the war years and registrations once again increased as the 1940s progressed, with over 700 new registrations in 1947. In the 1960s registrations surged, which is not always a good thing for a breed, but Whippet enthusiasts are thankfully a dedicated pack. In the last decade of the twentieth century, British registrations remained stable with between 1,431 and 1,747 Whippets registered annually, the latter figure a slight peak in 1996 although numbers subsequently dropped by a hundred or so.

In 1999 the Whippet Club celebrated its centenary year, holding an enormously well-supported show over a two-day period and encompassing all aspects of 'Whippetdom,' including obedience training,

A most famous Whippet is this Australian specimen known as Barna. It was owned by Joseph Brann and was the winner of the highest aggregate awarded by the Melbourne Metropolitan Kennel Club as well as many Whippet races.

agility and lure-coursing. The dog created primarily by the mining hands of the north, often described as 'a piece of canine art,' is indeed a breed of which to be proud.

THE WHIPPET IN TRACK RACING

In the nineteenth century, dog racing was definitely considered a 'working-class sport.' Because of this, more wealthy enthusiasts did not participate easily in the free and easy atmosphere that surrounded it. Although the Ladies Kennel Association held a Whippet race, honoured by the presence of King Edward and Queen Alexandra, this did not meet with the success that was hoped for.

Whippets used for both the track and for rabbit coursing needed to turn quickly and to be neat in using head and teeth. It

A scene from the turn of the century of a weigh-in prior to a Whippet race in England. Various races had weight standards because weight/height ratios impacted on stride lengths.

also was essential that they were capable of good speed. Those destined only for the track needed the power to get off quickly and, without interfering with the other runners, they had to move at speed to the end of the track.

Dogs frequently fought one another on the track and, on some tracks, canvas or nets were used

DID YOU KNOW?

Whippets have made their mark in many countries throughout the world. In 1980 Ch Beseeka Knight Errant of Silkstone won the award of Supreme Champion at the World Show, a highly prestigious event held in a different country each year.

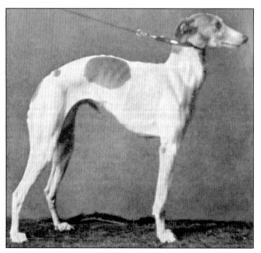

The Shirley prefix was very valued in Whippet circles during the 1930s. This photo depicts Mr J J Holgate's Shirley Dixie.

to divide the tracks so as to prevent this problem. On other tracks only string was used as a divider. A handicapping scale was used at most Championship events, usually dogs over 23 lbs, 23–18 lbs, 18–12 lbs and under 11 lbs. In 1888 White Eye, a black dog with one white eye, held the world record for 21-lb dogs, covering 200 yards in 12 seconds. Descriptions of these relatively early races are thoroughly informative with intriguing snippets of information, such as that the jump of an 18-lb dog could exceed 15 feet.

Much time, trouble and money were expended in getting a Whippet into the peak of condition for the track, for heavy

The famed Lottie Hampton, owned by Mr W Proctor, was greatly valued but did not have a successful show life in the 1930s.

DID YOU KNOW?

A great many countries have specialist Whippet clubs, such as South Africa's Whippet Club of Transvaal, founded in 1984. The Whippet Club of Canada was not founded until 1993, but before then there were several regional Whippet clubs in the country and there are plenty of Whippet speciality shows there.

betting took place so that efforts could prove worthwhile. Lancashire, in the north of England, was considered the home of Whippet racing and dogs from the county were thought to be of greater importance than those from elsewhere. Cinder tracks were faster than grass ones,

A famous British Whippet known as Ch Zanza Zanita was born in 1931 and died in 1933. During its very brief life span it won its championship and many other prizes including the three cups. This bitch was considered the best Whippet in 1933.

Another of Mr W Proctor's popular dogs was the Whippet known as Ch Manorley Mode.

and some tracks in Lancashire were known throughout the world.

At the starting line, each dog was held by the tail and the scruff of its neck. Hearing the starting pistol, the slipper would swing his dog forward and throw it as far as he could, hoping it would land on its feet. Clearly a good slipper gave the dog a great advantage! There was much shouting and yelling from onlookers, whilst at the other end of the track the dogs' owners shouted to their dogs, waving something at which their dog was to aim. That 'something' was usually a piece of material or a towel, but it was sometimes a dead rabbit or even a pigeon.

Will O' The Wisp of Mimosaland, bred by Mr W L Beard and owned by Mr Douglas Todd, was considered one of the very best Whippets of the 1930s, a dog that conformed closely to the standard of the time.

EARLY TRAINING OF RACING WHIPPETS

To train young Whippets, puppies were called to their food by waving a rag, setting the scene for when they were older. Roadwork could be between 12 and 20 miles each day, with the aim of perfecting feet and muscle tone. For strenuous exercise, a ball was used.

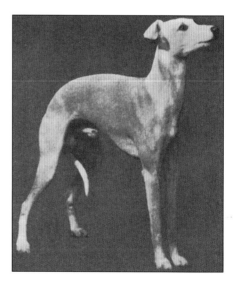

Mixed Fortune, an extremely typical Whippet whose show career in 1933 was very successful, was owned and exhibited by Mr Arthur Honeybone of Wallingford, Berks.

Many Whippets were said to have eaten better food than their owners. Some of the best dogs were fed only on Scotch beef, sent down from Scotland especially for them because the local beef was not believed sufficiently good. Diet was carefully controlled, and some dogs were muzzled so that they were prevented from eating food not intended for them. Many were kept almost entirely in the dark except when being raced, and they were fed and attended to only by one person, so depriving them of what today would be considered essential companionship. In other respects these highly prized dogs were treated with kindness, but standards of canine care then were not as they are today.

Two portraits of Zanza Zanita, photographed by two different photographers in 1933.

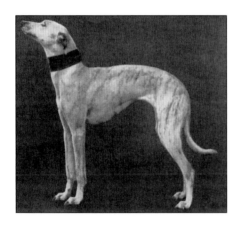

Left, top: A New Zealand Whippet named Bonny Argyle was a top winner in the 1930s.
Left, bottom: Sandbloom was a beloved pet for Miss Robinson, representing a 'pet-quality' dog from the period.

A successful dog was always the centre of love and affection in the family, and often a family was actually supported by the winnings of the dog. Many unsuccessful dogs did not live out their natural lives, for poor men could not afford to keep bad stock. On the other hand, a good dog, too old for racing, often lived the rest of its life by the family fire.

TRICKS OF THE TRADE
Because money was involved in Whippet racing, a number of

tricks were practised regularly. Often a dog from another district was known by name, but not by sight, so a good dog could find itself entered under the name of an inferior one, playing havoc with the handicap system! An aid to those involved in such misdemeanours was that the dogs were kept well rugged-up until the moment the race commenced, so with skill even colour could be changed and the deed concealed. There was even a case of a dog being entered as a bitch!

Sometimes 'holding' was employed, so that a dog was not slipped immediately at the sound of the gun. In fact, it was known for the pistol to go off and not one of the Whippets to be released from the slips. This was because each man slipping was betting on another's dog. It was by no means unknown for a dog to have one of its feet trodden to cause lameness. Even school children had a vested interest in the sport, for they were frequently quizzed by their teachers about which dogs would win.

WHIPPETS IN AMERICA

In America the Whippet was recognised in 1888, and a white dog with brown and yellow markings named Jack Dempsey was registered in the American Kennel Club's (AKC's) Stud Book that same year under the 'Miscellaneous' heading. A bitch by the name of Boston Model was the first Whippet known to have won well at a dog show, taking first prize in a mixed breed class in 1893. Of course there have been many great kennels in America through the decades since then, the first of which was 'Bay View,' making its public appearance in the Whippet world in 1903. In 1904 Bay View Pride, whelped in

This Whippet, Lady Beatrice, was bred by Mr Boothe in Moose Jaw, Canada, in 1928. It was the first Whippet sent to Japan where it became the prized possession of Miss A Wada and formed the base for the production of further Whippets in Japan.

The Standard Manchester Terrier, a Whippet relative, once excelled in a different kind of race: a contest of killing rats, of which the Manchester was an immodest winner.

19

1902, became the first American champion. The only Whippet to win the famed Westminster Kennel Club Dog Show was Ch Courtenay Fleetfoot of Pennyworth, owned by Penny Worth Kennels, in 1964. The most famous American kennel in modern times is Sporting Fields,

This 1933 champion known as Ch Sparkle of Tytterton was owned by Mrs Critchley Salmonson and was bred by K Henley.

WHIPPETS IN AUSTRALIA

It is likely that even in the nineteenth century some settlers in Australia took their Whippets with them, and Whippet racing was certainly recorded in 1869. However, not until the twentieth

Thistle Down of YNYS was a bitch bred by Mr H May in 1931. It had its name changed when Mrs R Barry Adams bought it. It was then known as Miss Thistle Doone

whose dogs dominate most of the shows in the US.

Although Whippets at general shows usually enjoy greater popularity in Britain than in America, at breed specialty shows numbers exhibited have reached phenomenal figures—over 500 on occasions. It is interesting to note that the proportion of judges in America who are breed specialists is small in comparison with breed specialist judges at shows in the UK.

Brilliant Sand, a brindle bitch, won many firsts in Open Shows and was owned by Mr W C Taylor. Its beautiful clean body was exemplary of the breed in the early 1930s.

History

The Channel Island champion was Mrs W J de Gruchy's Memory Star. Amongst her many prizes was a Best in Show in 1934.

Ch Calpin Bartic's Best in Show win at Brisbane Royal in 1951.

WHIPPETS IN EUROPE

In Scandinavia, Whippets were shown as long ago as 1900, and in about 1917 Queen Maude of Norway imported two Whippets to Norway, giving certain notoriety to the breed. As in other countries, many Scandinavian enthusiasts are seriously

Born in July 1928, Silver Lightning was an exceptionally fast runner and won numerous prizes and sired many champions. Many fast running Whippets are also successful show dogs.

century were Whippets bred specifically for the show ring.

British imported stock has had a great influence on the Whippet scene in Australia, in part because of quarantine laws in the UK, making it easier to import from Britain than from elsewhere. Several Whippets have won high awards at prestigious shows here, one early such achievement being

dedicated to their breed and the *Svenska Whipptklubben* (Swedish Whippet Club) was formed in 1976.

The Whippet scene in continental Europe is somewhat different again, France being the country on the European mainland in which the breed is most popular. A French breed club was formed in the late 1940s and the breed club shows attract

Ch Silver Knight was a fawn and white dog, born in 1930. He was a consistent winner at the shows.

21

substantial entries. However, although a goodly number of Whippets are registered in France each year, many of these are destined for pet homes rather than the show ring.

In Germany, Whippets were first registered in 1903 but in those early years there was not always a clear defining line between large Italian Greyhounds and Whippets. Until the war years, several British-bred Whippets were imported to

The antique collars worn by champion runners of yore are coming back into fashion for modern-day champions.

Flying Imp, owned by J Cahill, celebrated his first birthday by winning the Napier Whippet Puppy Cup in Australia. He also won the Wellington Cup in the most important North Island race, running 200 yards in slightly over 12 seconds.

Germany but today the breed is not greatly popular there, with registration numbers being similar to those in Switzerland, despite the disparity in size and population between the two countries.

THE SHOW SCENE IN BRITAIN TODAY

Although many breeds have significantly higher Kennel Club registration figures, the number of Whippets exhibited at shows usually far exceeds most others. There are generally upward of 200 Whippets entered at a show, often nearer to 250 and sometimes beyond, such as at Crufts in 1999 when there were 335 Whippets, making a total of 374 entries. Such high numbers sometimes necessitate two judges, one for

dogs and another for bitches. To win consistently amongst such strong competition is not an easy task. Many Whippet people enjoy the breed for its own sake, whether or not they achieve high honours in the show ring.

Whippets prove obedient and elegant in the show ring. This handler and Whippet are making a very professional showing.

Whippets excel in Britain's show rings today and are represented by strong entries. Not only is the number of dogs entered high but also the quality of the dogs is consistent and impressive.

23

Upon viewing this elegant creature, who could query the Whippet being described as 'a piece of canine art'? Nothing is nearer to the truth. A well-constructed Whippet is a truly beautiful animal with grace displayed in every movement, whether speeding across a field, investigating the garden or reclining comfortably on the sofa or bed. The breed's graceful lines are clearly seen thanks to the smooth coat, making a feast for the eyes of any true lover of sight hounds.

The Whippet is a highly adaptable dog and can fit in well with most household situations. His size, short coat and clean habits make him easy to have around and a pleasure to keep.

PERSONALITY

The Whippet is a wonderful companion dog; it is an affectionate, gentle and faithful breed with an even temper and quiet disposition. Having said that, Whippets are very quick and, particularly as youngsters, are quite capable of dashing off for some important purpose they have in mind (often connected with food). This means that an owner has to keep a careful eye on his Whippet's surroundings.

Whippets adore human company and most are all too happy to snuggle up on your lap when given the opportunity, even if you are lying on a garden sun-bed in the heat of the day. Most Whippets do seem to be sun worshippers, and undoubtedly enjoy both heat and comfort. There is also many a Whippet that sleeps under the duvet of his owner's bed, providing warmth and companionship for those who allow it (and admit to it). It has to be said that in bed a Whippet is rather like an animated hot-water bottle!

WHIPPETS AND OTHER PETS

Because of their nature, some Whippets do not take kindly to cats and other small creatures, so sensible management is prudent if introducing a Whippet to the family cat or vice versa. A Whippet must be taught to know the rules of the household, and that does not involve chasing the family feline. Cats, though, seem to sense which dogs they need to respect and which they do not, which helps what might otherwise, perhaps, be a slightly difficult situation.

DID YOU KNOW?

Although considered a relatively new creation as a specific breed, dogs similar to those we know today as Whippets have been around for many a long year. In 1841 such dogs were described as 'a dog bred betwixt a greyhound and a spaniel.' But referring back to a dictionary of 1550, the word 'whippet' was described as 'a lively young woman; a light wench.'

Of course, the majority of Whippets, if socialised carefully with other family pets from an early age, is able to live alongside them in perfect harmony. Many a Whippet and cat form firm friendships and become almost inseparable. However, even though your Whippet may have accepted the family cat, the same sentiment does not likely apply when a neighbour's cat has the audacity to venture into your garden!

WHIPPETS WITH CHILDREN
The parent of both dogs and children must teach the latter to respect their canine friends and to treat them gently. Whippets are tolerant dogs and most thoroughly enjoy the company of children, especially if they have been

A living work of art, the Whippet is an elegant dog, seemingly aloof, but actually a wonderful companion.

The author and her niece take their Whippet on long walks into the countryside.

sensibly introduced whilst the dog is still young. Nonetheless, one should always keep in mind that Whippets, like all other dogs, appreciate some peace and quiet and that the limits of their tolerance should never be put to the test. Careful supervision is the key to building up a successful relationship between child and dog.

SIZE
Whippets might be considered of medium size, their height ranging between 44 and 51 cms (17.5–20 ins), bitches being the smaller of the two sexes as in most breeds. However, this is not a heavy breed because of its fine construction, so actual weight is considerably less than most other breeds that attain this height. This means that Whippets can be picked up with relative ease when necessary.

Because of their long legs, Whippets not only can move fast but also have an ability to reach up to things that one might naively consider to be out of

Adaptable and affectionate, Whippets fit into all families.

reach. Tasty morsels left on kitchen units are by no means beyond their grasp, and it can be rather amusing to see a Whippet do a quick circuit of the kitchen units, stretching up on its hind legs to see what might be available for the take!

Sometimes a Whippet's long legs seem to stretch out endlessly when reclining, so one must take care not to sit on them accidentally, especially if concealed under some cosy item of your furnishings.

LIFESPAN

Clearly, when taking a Whippet into your home, the ultimate aim will be that the dog remains with you for life. A healthy Whippet can be expected to live on average for around 14 years, but many enjoy a much longer lifespan. It is

Enjoying a rest in the sun, this Whippet has been alerted to a sharp sound. Note his ears in the prick position.

27

Whippets make reliable watchdogs, but they are more curious than most other dogs.

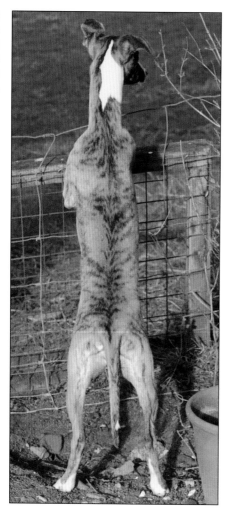

The colours of this breed are many and varied, and there is no preference for any colour. So it is that Whippets are found in a wide variety of hues, ranging from white through to black, with brindles and parti-colours mixed in for further variety. This array of colours is just another interesting aspect of this delightful breed. Of course some people will have personal preferences regarding colour, and in some breeding lines a particular colour appears more frequently than others, but selection should certainly never be made on colour alone.

The skin of the Whippet is fine and, without the protection of a long coat, can mark and tear rather easily. This should be borne in mind when selecting areas for a Whippet's free run.

HEALTH CONSIDERATIONS
Although basically a healthy breed, like all dogs, some Whippets do suffer from

not at all unusual to come across some moderately sprightly Whippets at 16 years of age.

SKIN, COAT AND COLOUR
A Whippet's coat is fine, short and close in texture, so can be kept easily under control with simple grooming and general care.

DID YOU KNOW?

To take a urine sample to your veterinary surgeon for analysis, the easiest way is to catch the urine in a large, clean bowl or jug and then transfer this to a bottle. Owners attempting to get their dogs or bitches to urinate directly into a bottle will spend many fruitless hours in their efforts!

DID YOU KNOW?

In the early decades of the twentieth century, obstacle races were introduced for racing Whippets. However, although these were greatly popular with audiences, the dogs seemed to enjoy them less. Indeed in the first race only one Whippet made it to the end, the other five failed to finish!

FEELING THE COLD

In part because of their thin skin and their low proportion of body fat, Whippets do feel the cold more than many other dogs. They need to wear warm coats when outside in cold weather. They also seem rather susceptible to cold winds. It is also important that any special canine bedding in the house is kept away from draughts, so therefore should be raised slightly off the ground.

'I found a Whippet in my bed when I awoke!' Puppies are great companions for children.

illnesses and it is only fair to owners and to the dogs in question that attention is brought to these. Awareness of any problems that may possibly arise can only help owners to know when it is necessary to seek veterinary advice.

ANAESTHESIA SENSITIVITY

Whippets, like other sight hounds, have a very low proportion of body fat in relation to their size. As a result, anaesthesia is one of various medications to which Whippets are sensitive, so it is important to discuss this with your veterinary surgeon prior to surgery taking place. A special anaesthetic that is more suitable for this and other similar breeds can be used, and it is recommended that barbiturates be avoided.

Whippets cannot tolerate the cold. This dog will not even sit in the snow.

Whippets want to be with their owners at all times. They are very devoted pets.

OBESITY

Most Whippets love their food, and especially as they progress toward old age may well put on excess fat. All Whippets, especially older ones, should always be kept trim and there are really no adequate excuses for not noticing that one's Whippet is

Given the choice, Whippets prefer to sleep with their loved ones.

putting on too much weight, for even without the scales every extra pound or kilo of weight seems to show!

DENTAL HEALTH

Although Whippets usually have strong teeth, it is always important to pay close attention to the care of teeth and gums. This way they will remain as healthy

as possible with consequent prevention of decay, infection and resultant loss of teeth.

Infection in the gums may not just stop there. The bacteria from such infection is carried through the bloodstream, the result of which can be disease of liver, kidney, heart and joints. This is all the more reason to realise that efficient dental care is of utmost importance throughout any dog's life.

Sunburn

Because Whippets love the sun so much, care should be taken that the sun does not burn their rather delicate skin, especially on the muzzle. A little gentle sun cream can be applied on the muzzle of Whippets who really do insist on lying outside too long. Obviously owners should encourage their dogs inside the house or to a shady spot for cooling off from time to time, and it is easy to tell when they are really getting too hot because they pant visibly.

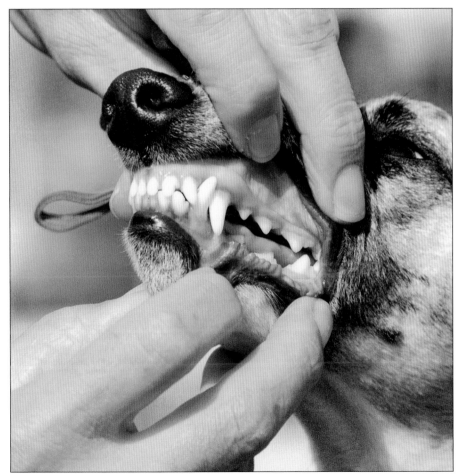

Whippets have strong teeth but their health should be monitored regularly. A thorough examination (by you) once a month is sufficient; the vet will confirm your findings during the Whippet's regular checkups.

WHIPPET

The Kennel Club breed standard for the Whippet is effectively a 'blue-print' for the breed. It sets down the various points of the dog in words, enabling a visual picture to be conjured up in the mind of the reader. However, this is more easily said than done. Not only do standards vary from country to country, but people's interpretations of breed standards vary also. It is this difference of interpretation that makes judges select

How each dog measures up in the show ring is based on the breed standard, the blueprint of the ideal Whippet.

different dogs for top honours, for their opinions differ as to which dog most closely fits the breed standard. That is not to say that a good dog does not win regularly under different judges, nor that an inferior dog may rarely even be placed at a show, at least not amongst quality competition.

The breed standard given here in full is that authorised by the English Kennel Club. It is reasonably comprehensive and so is fairly self-explanatory. However, as is the case with most breeds, there are variances between the standard used in Britain and that in other parts of the world. The differences between the English standard and the American Kennel Club (AKC) standard are particularly worth mention. The AKC standard is longer, as is the case for many breeds, and so encompasses a little more clarity and depth in certain aspects. Certainly the AKC's description of 'General Appearance' is, I feel, worthy of quotation for it is of interest to devotees of the breed throughout the world, not just in the USA:

'A medium size sighthound giving the appearance of elegance and fitness, denoting great speed, power and balance without coarse-ness. A true sporting hound that covers a maximum of distance with a minimum of lost motion. Should convey an impression of beautifully balanced muscular power and strength, combined with great elegance and grace of outline. Symmetry of outline, muscular development and powerful gait are the main consid-erations; the dog being built for speed and work, all forms of exaggeration should be avoided.'

An important difference between the two standards is that of height. In America the specifica-tions for height are: dogs, 19–22 ins (48–56 cms), and bitches, 18–21 ins (46–53 cms), both sexes being allowed greater height than that of the English standard. However, in the USA, Whippets that are more than half an inch below or above the stipulated heights are disqualified.

It will also be noticed that in the English standard there is no reference to actual eye colour, but in America yellow or light eyes are to be strictly penalised, whilst blue or wall eyes are reason for disqual-ification. Another interesting further inclusion in the American standard is that fully pigmented eyelids are desirable.

Because of the Whippet's delicate skin, it is not uncommon for dogs in show rings throughout the world to exhibit scars, and I hope no understanding judges

penalise these. However, the American standard goes so far as to say, 'Old scars and injuries, the result of work or accident, should not be allowed to prejudice the dog's chance in the show ring.'

Although one could discuss the differences for many more pages than the text of this book will allow, it is time to move on to the standard as issued by The Kennel Club.

The judge at a dog show determines how well your Whippet conforms to the breed standard. The dog that most closely conforms is deemed Best of Breed.

THE KENNEL CLUB STANDARD FOR THE WHIPPET

General Appearance: Balanced combination of muscular power and strength with elegance and grace of outline. Built for speed and work. All forms of exaggeration should be avoided.

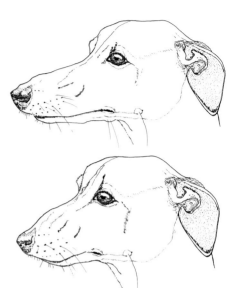

The Whippet's outline is marked by grace and elegance.

The uppermost figure illustrates a Whippet with a correct muzzle. The lower figure illustrates a Whippet with a muzzle that is too short.

Characteristics: An ideal companion. Highly adaptable in domestic and sporting surroundings.

Temperament: Gentle, affectionate, even disposition.

Head and Skull: Long and lean, flat on top, tapering to muzzle with slight stop, rather wide between the eyes, jaws powerful and clean-cut, nose black, in blues a bluish colour permitted, liver nose in creams and other dilute colours, in whites or parti-colours a butterfly nose permissible.

Eyes: Oval, bright, expression very alert.

Ears: Rose shaped, small, fine in texture.

Mouth: Jaws strong with a perfect, regular and complete scissor bite, i.e. upper teeth closely overlapping lower teeth and set square to the jaws.

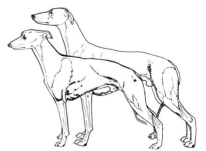

A Whippet (foreground) compared to a Greyhound.

Body too short and square.

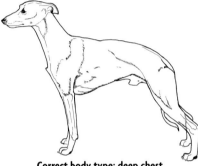

Correct body type: deep chest and long, strong back.

in front. Brisket deep. Broad, well muscled back, firm, somewhat long, showing graceful arch over the loin but not humped. Ribs well sprung. Loin giving impression of strength and power. Definite tuck up.

Hindquarters: Strong, broad across thighs, with well developed second thighs. Stifles well bent without exaggeration with hocks well let down. Able to stand naturally over a lot of ground.

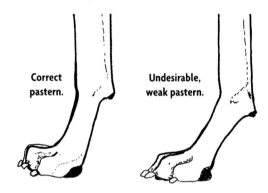

Correct pastern.

Undesirable, weak pastern.

Neck: Long, muscular, elegantly arched.

Forequarters: Shoulders well laid back with flat muscles. Moderate space between the shoulder blades at the withers. The upper arm is approximately of equal length to the shoulder, placed so that the elbow falls directly under the withers when viewed in profile. Forearms straight and upright with moderate bladed bone. Front not too wide. Pasterns strong with slight spring.

Body: Chest very deep with plenty of heart room. Well filled

Feet: Oval, well split up between toes, knuckles well arched, pads thick, nails strong.

Tail: No feathering. Long, tapering, reaching at least to the hock. When in action carried in a delicate curve not higher than the back.

Gait/Movement: Should possess great freedom of action. In profile should move with a long, easy stride whilst holding topline. The

Whippet

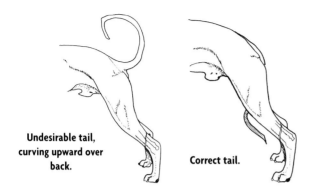

Undesirable tail, curving upward over back.

Correct tail.

forelegs should be thrown forward and low over the ground. Hind legs should come well under the body giving greater propelling power. General movement not to look stilted, high stepping, short or mincing. True coming and going.

Coat: Fine, short, close in texture.

Colour: Any colour or mixture of colours.

Size: Height: dogs: 47–51 cms (18.5–20 ins); bitches: 44–47 cms (17.5–18.5 ins).

Outer figure shows correct forequarters. Inner figure illustrates a dog that is too broad in front.

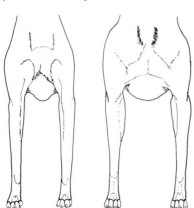

Faults: Any departure from the foregoing points should be considered a fault and the seriousness with which the fault should be regarded should be in exact proportion to its degree and its effect upon the health and welfare of the dog.

Note: Male animals should have two apparently normal testicles fully descended into the scrotum.

Although a great deal can be learned from the breed standard, only by seeing good quality, typical specimens can one really learn to appreciate the breed's merits. Therefore, readers interested in showing their Whippets should watch other dogs being exhibited and learn as much as possible from established breeders and exhibitors. Personally, I have found Whippet exhibitors to be a most helpful and dedicated bunch of people, so undoubtedly there are many people out there who are willing to give advice and assistance to a newcomer.

It is helpful to attend specialist breed seminars when available. Here the finer points of the breed can be explained fully and discussed. There is usually a dog, or perhaps a handful, available for demonstration purposes, and there may be an opportunity for participants to gain hands-on experience, giving a valuable insight into the structure of the animal.

The Whippet is a breed built both for speed and for work, and good-quality specimens should easily portray this. They need to be well muscled, but that muscle should be hard and flat, not overly bulging as is more appropriate for some heavier breeds.

Because of the Whippet's work as a hunting dog, the neck is important and we can see from the standard that it is to be long, muscular and arched. A Whippet with a long neck must, of necessity, have correct shoulder lay-back, without which the head can simply not be carried as it should. Faults in shoulder construction also play havoc with movement, as do so many other important aspects of a dog's physical make-up.

It would be all too easy to take each part of the beautiful Whippet and explain in depth why it should be as it is, but this is not a book designed for that purpose. However, it must be brought to your attention that the chest is to be deep and the ribs well sprung, thus allowing sufficient heart room; this is a breed that needs both heart and lung capacity to perform its natural function in life.

Although there is an arch over the loin, this, like the rest of the dog, should not be exaggerated, and therefore should not form a hump as is occasionally seen. The outline of the Whippet is one that flows gracefully. Again, because of this breed's function it must be capable of driving from the hindquarters and the construction is well

A proud junior handler shows off her well-trained Whippet.

described in the standard.

Prior to the current standard, effective from 2006 when The Kennel Club revised this standard, the standard had changed once in over 40 years. One of the previous standards, having been drawn up in 1945, was a very valuable standard; an important sentence included was that '...forelegs should be thrown forward and low over the ground like a thoroughbred horse, not a Hackney-like action...'

The 1945 standard also gave a lower 'ideal' height and listed a large number of faults, which is interesting to read and absorb. But of course judges should certainly not 'fault judge'; their appraisal of each exhibit should be that of the composite whole, not merely the faults of each dog.

The Whippet is a breed of great beauty, combining muscular power, strength, elegance and grace, and should be unexaggerated in any way. Long may it remain thus.

WHIPPET

Puppies with future show careers should have their mouths handled daily to accustom them to this inspection.

OWNER CONSIDERATIONS

You have probably decided on a Whippet as your choice of pet following a visit to the home of a friend or acquaintance, where you have seen a graceful Whippet wandering quietly around the house and taking its ease in designated, comfortable places. However, as a new owner you must realise that a good deal of care, commitment and careful training goes into raising a boisterous puppy so that your pet turns into a well-behaved adult.

In deciding to take on a new puppy you will be committing yourself to around 14 years of responsibility. No dog should be discarded after a few months, or even a few years, after the novelty has worn off. Instead, your Whippet should be joining your household to spend the rest of its days with you.

Although temperamentally a Whippet is fairly easy to look after, you will still need to carry out a certain amount of training. This needs to be firm, so that your dog knows exactly who is in control, but to produce the most efficient results training should not be overly strict.

A Whippet generally likes to

be clean around the house, but you will need to teach your puppy what is and is not expected. You will need to be consistent in your instructions; it is no good accepting certain behaviour one day and not the next. Not only will your puppy simply not understand, he will be utterly confused. Your Whippet will want to please you, so you will need to demonstrate clearly how your puppy is to achieve this.

The dog you are taking into your home will be only of medium size, but will have what sometimes appear to be extraordinarily long legs. These, coupled with a long neck, long muzzle and keen eyesight, provide an opportunity for plenty of mischief if your dog sees fit! You may wish to consider erecting baby gates so that your new hound is restricted to certain areas of the house. That will work at least for the time being, although your Whippet may soon learn to jump them! There will undoubtedly be a period of training and settling, a period during which you may have needed to rearrange some of your household items so that nothing will cause injury, or get broken.

Whatever the problems encountered, this will be a period of great fun, but you must be prepared for mishaps around the home during the first few weeks of your lives together. It will be important that precious ornaments are kept well out of harm's way, and you will have to think twice about where you place hot cups of coffee or anything breakable. Accidents can and do happen, so you will need to think ahead to prevent these. Electric cables must be carefully concealed, and your puppy must be taught where and where not to go.

Before making your commitment to a new puppy, do also think carefully about your future holiday plans. Depending on the country in which you live, your dog may or may not be able to travel abroad with

The love of the race is a natural instinct for Whippet puppies. New owners are advised to limit the 'horse play' until their Whippets have developed their limbs completely.

you. Thanks to the advent of the PETS Passport Scheme, travelling with your dog is becoming more common. If you have thought things through carefully, discussed the matter thoroughly with all close family members, hopefully you will have come to the right decision. If you decide that a Whippet should join your family, this will hopefully be a happy, long-term relationship for all parties concerned.

BUYING A WHIPPET PUPPY

Although you may be looking for a Whippet as a pet, rather than a show dog, this does not mean that you want a dog that is in any way 'second-rate.' A caring breeder will have brought up the entire litter of puppies with the same amount of dedication, and a puppy destined for a pet home should be just as healthy as one that hopes to end up in the show ring, or indeed on the race track.

Because you have carefully selected this breed, you will want a Whippet that is a typical specimen, both in looks and in temperament. In your endeavours to find such a puppy you will have to select the breeder with care. The Kennel Club will

almost certainly be able to give you the name of a contact within the breed club. Through the club, you can probably be put in touch with breeders, but to obtain the breeder of your choice you may have to put down your name on a waiting list. It is important that you have done your homework carefully, so that you feel both breed and breeder are right for you.

Even though you are probably not looking for a show dog, it is always a good idea to visit a show so that you can see

quality specimens of the breed. This will also give you an opportunity to meet breeders who will probably be able to answer some of your queries. In addition you will get some idea about which breeders appear to take most care of their stock, and which are likely to have given their puppies the best possible start in life.

When buying your puppy, you will need to know about vaccinations, those already given and those due. It is important that any injections already given by a veterinary surgeon have documentary evidence to prove this. A worming routine is also vital for any young puppy, so the breeder should be able to tell you exactly what treatment has been given, when it has been administered and how you should continue.

Clearly when selecting a puppy, the one you choose

must be in good condition. The coat should look healthy and there should be no discharge from eyes or nose. Ears should also be clean, and of course there should be absolutely no sign of parasites. Check that there is no rash on the skin, and of course the puppy you choose should not have evidence of loose motions.

Finally, a few words of advice. Always insist that you see the puppy's dam and, if possible, the sire. However, frequently the sire will not be owned by the breeder of the litter, but a photograph may be available for you to see. Ask if the breeder has any other of the puppy's relations that you could meet. For example, there may be an older half-sister or half-brother and it would be interesting for you to see how he/she has turned out, the eventual size, overall quality, temperament and so on.

Be sure, too, that if you decide to buy a puppy, all relevant documentation is provided at the time of sale. You will need a copy of the pedigree, preferably Kennel Club registration documents, vaccination certificates and a feeding chart so that you know exactly how the puppy has been fed and how you should continue. Some careful breeders provide their puppy buyers

DID YOU KNOW?

Your selection of a good puppy can be determined by your needs. A show potential or a good pet? It is your choice. Every puppy, however,

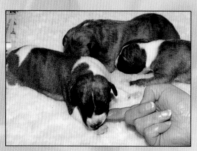

should be of good temperament. Although show-quality puppies are bred and raised with emphasis on physical conformation, responsible breeders strive for equally good temperament. Do not buy from a breeder who concentrates solely on physical beauty at the expense of personality.

with a small amount of food. This prevents the risk of an upset tummy, allowing for a gradual change of diet if that particular brand of food is not locally available.

COMMITMENT OF OWNERSHIP

After considering all of these factors, you have most likely already made some very important decisions about selecting your puppy. You have chosen a Whippet, which means that you have decided which characteristics you want in a dog and what type of dog will best fit into your family and lifestyle. If you have selected a breeder, you have gone a step further—you have done your research and found a responsible, conscientious person who breeds quality Whippets and who should be a reliable source of help as you and your puppy adjust to life together. If you have observed a litter in action, you have obtained a firsthand look at the dynamics of a puppy 'pack' and, thus, you should learn about each pup's individual personality—perhaps you have even found one that particularly appeals to you.

However, even if you have not yet found the Whippet puppy of your dreams, observing pups will help you learn to recognise certain

behaviour and to determine what a pup's behaviour indicates about his temperament. You will be able to pick out which pups are the leaders, which ones are less outgoing, which ones are confident, which ones are shy, playful,

INSURANCE

The Kennel Club will offer you free insurance for the first few weeks when you transfer ownership of your

puppy, allowing you to take up the policy when this expires. If you own a pet dog, it is sensible to take out such a policy as veterinary fees can be high, although routine vaccinations and boosters are not covered. Look carefully at the many options open to you before deciding which suits you best.

DOCUMENTATION

Two important documents you will get from the breeder are the pup's pedigree and registration papers. The breeder should register the litter and each pup with The Kennel Club, and it is necessary for you to have the paperwork to transfer ownership to yourself. If you are purchasing

a pup that is not eligible for the Breed Register, you can still register your pup on the Activity Register, which will enable you to compete in competitions licensed by The Kennel Club, i.e. Obedience, Working Trials, Agility, Heelwork to Music and Flyball. You will not be able to show your dog or be eligible to compete in Field Trials or Gundog Working Tests.

friendly, aggressive, etc. Equally as important, you will learn to recognise what a healthy pup should look and act like. All of these things will help you in your search, and when you find the Whippet that was meant for you, you will know it!

Researching your breed, selecting a responsible breeder and observing as many pups as possible are all important steps on the way to dog ownership. It may seem like a lot of effort...and you have not even taken the pup home yet! Remember, though, you cannot be too careful when it comes to deciding on the type of dog you want and finding out about your prospective pup's background. Buying a puppy is not—or should not be—just another whimsical purchase. This is one instance in which you actually do get to choose your own family! You may be thinking that buying a puppy should be fun—it should not be so serious and so much work. Keep in mind that your puppy is not a cuddly stuffed toy or decorative lawn ornament, but a creature that will become a real member of your family. You will come to realise that, whilst buying a puppy is a pleasurable and exciting endeavour, it is not something to be taken lightly. Relax...the fun will start when the pup comes home!

Always keep in mind that a puppy is nothing more than a baby in a furry disguise...a baby who is virtually helpless in a human world and who trusts his owner for fulfilment of his basic needs for survival. In addition to water and shelter, your pup needs care, protection, guidance and love. If you are not prepared to commit to this, then you are not prepared to own a dog.

Wait a minute, you say. How hard could this be? All of my neighbours own dogs and they seem to be doing just fine. Why should I have to worry about all of this? Well, you should not worry about it; in fact, you will probably find that once your Whippet pup gets used to his new home, he will fall into his place in the family quite naturally. But it never hurts to emphasise the commitment of dog ownership. With some time

DID YOU KNOW?

Breeders rarely release puppies until they are eight to ten weeks of age. This is an acceptable age for most

breeds of dog, excepting toy breeds, which are not released until around 12 weeks, given their petite sizes. If a breeder has a puppy that is 12 weeks or more, it is likely well socialised and house-trained. Be sure that it is otherwise healthy before deciding to take it home.

These Whippet puppies are only a few days old. Their eyes haven't opened yet and they are completely dependent on their mother for everything.

and patience, it is really not too difficult to raise a curious and exuberant Whippet pup to be a well-adjusted and well-mannered adult dog—a dog that could be your most loyal friend.

PREPARING PUPPY'S PLACE IN YOUR HOME

Researching your breed and finding a breeder are only two

Whippets remain puppylike for their first few years of life. When puppy-proofing your home, make choices that will endure a few years' worth of Whippet exuberance.

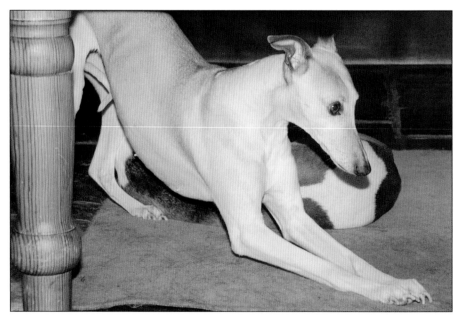

aspects of the 'homework' you will have to do before bringing your Whippet puppy home. You will also have to prepare your home and family for the new addition. Much as you would prepare a nursery for a newborn baby, you will need to designate

YOUR SCHEDULE...

If you lead an erratic, unpredictable life, with daily or weekly changes in your work requirements, consider the problems of owning a puppy. The new puppy has to be fed regularly, socialised (loved, petted, handled, introduced to other people) and, most importantly, allowed to visit outdoors for toilet training. As the dog gets older, it can be more tolerant of deviations in its feeding and toilet relief.

a place in your home that will be the puppy's own. How you prepare your home will depend on how much freedom the dog will be allowed. Whatever you decide, you must ensure that he has a place that he can 'call his own.'

When you bring your new puppy into your home, you are bringing him into what will become his home as well. Obviously, you did not buy a puppy so that he could take over your house, but in order for a puppy to grow into a stable, well-adjusted dog, he has to feel comfortable in his surroundings. Remember, he is leaving the warmth and security of his mother and littermates, as well as the familiarity of the only place he has ever known, so it is important to make his transition as easy as possible. By

preparing a place in your home for the puppy, you are making him feel as welcome as possible in a strange new place. It should not take him long to get used to it, but the sudden shock of being transplanted is somewhat traumatic for a young pup. Imagine how a small child would feel in the same situation—that is how your puppy must be feeling. It is up to you to reassure him and to let him know, 'Little chap, you are going to like it here!'

WHAT YOU SHOULD BUY

CRATE
To someone unfamiliar with the use of crates in dog training, it

Sometimes new owners mistakenly believe that adopting two Whippet puppies will remedy the situation of a lonely single pup if the owners are not home all day. Two untrained, unattended Whippet puppies are easily *five* times the trouble!

PHOTO COURTESY OF DOSKOCIL.

Your local pet shop should have a wide variety of crates to show you. A medium-size crate is suitable for the puppy and full-grown Whippet.

humane and highly effective uses in dog care and training. For example, crate training is a very popular and very successful house-training method. A crate can keep your dog safe during travel; and, perhaps most importantly, a crate provides your dog with a place of his own in your home. It serves as a 'doggie bedroom' of sorts—your Whippet can curl up in his crate when he wants to sleep or when he just needs a break. Many dogs sleep in their crates overnight. When lined with soft bedding and with his favourite toy placed inside, a crate becomes a cosy pseudo-den for your dog. Like his ancestors, he too will seek out the comfort and retreat of a den—you just happen to be providing him with something a little more luxurious than his early ancestors enjoyed.

As far as purchasing a crate, the type that you buy is up to you. It will most likely be one of the two most popular types: wire or fibreglass. There are advantages and disadvantages to each type. For example, a wire crate is more open, allowing the air to flow through and affording the dog a view of what is going on around him whilst a fibreglass crate is sturdier. Both can double as travel crates, providing protection for the dog. The size of the crate is

may seem like punishment to shut a dog in a crate, but this is not the case at all. Although all breeders do not advocate crate training, more and more breeders and trainers are recommending crates as a preferred tool for show puppies as well as pet puppies. Crates are not cruel—crates have many

another thing to consider. Puppies do not stay puppies forever—in fact, sometimes it seems as if they grow right before your eyes. A Yorkie-sized crate may be fine for a very young Whippet pup, but it will not do him much good for long! Unless you have the money and the inclination to buy a new crate every time your pup has a growth spurt, it is better to get one that will accommodate your dog both as a pup and at full size. A medium-size crate will be necessary for a full-grown Whippet, who stands approximately 20 inches high.

BEDDING

Veterinary bedding in the dog's crate will help the dog feel more at home and you may also like to pop in a small blanket. This will take the place of the leaves, twigs, etc., that the pup would use in the wild to make a den; the pup can make his own

'burrow' in the crate. Although your pup is far removed from his den-making ancestors, the denning instinct is still a part of his genetic makeup. Second, until you bring your pup home, he has been sleeping amidst the warmth of his mother and litter-mates, and whilst a blanket is not the same as a warm, breathing body, it still provides heat and something with which to snuggle. You will want to wash your pup's

Wire crates are ideal for the active Whippet who always needs to see what's going on about him. The wire crate also provides the best ventilation.

BOY OR GIRL?

An important consideration to be discussed is the sex of your puppy. For a family companion, a bitch may be the better choice, considering the female's inbred concern for all young creatures and her accompanying tolerance and patience. It is always advisable to spay a pet bitch, which may guarantee her a longer life.

49

CRATE TRAINING TIPS

During crate training, you should partition off the section of the crate in which the pup stays. If he is given too big an area, this will hinder your training efforts. Crate training is based on the fact that a

dog does not like to soil his sleeping quarters, so it is ineffective to keep a pup in a crate that is so big that he can relieve himself in one end and get far enough away from it to sleep. Also, you want to make the crate den-like for the pup. Blankets and a favourite toy will make the crate cosy for the small pup; as he grows, you may want to evict some of his 'roommates' to make more room.

It will take some coaxing at first, but be patient. Given some time to get used to it, your pup will adapt to his new home-within-a-home quite nicely.

Purchase top-quality rope toys that are constructed of nylon not cotton. Nylon rope toys are more expensive but outlast cotton many times over.

bedding frequently in case he has an accident in his crate, and replace or remove any blanket that becomes ragged and starts to fall apart.

Toys

Toys are a must for dogs of all ages, especially for curious playful pups. Puppies are the 'children' of the dog world, and what child does not love toys? Chew toys provide enjoyment to both dog and owner—your dog will enjoy playing with his favourite toys, whilst you will enjoy the fact that they distract him from your expensive shoes and leather sofa. Puppies love to chew; in fact, chewing is a physical need for pups as they are teething, and everything looks appetising! The full range of your possessions—from old tea towel to Oriental carpet— are fair game in the eyes of a teething pup. Puppies are not all that discerning when it comes to finding something to literally 'sink their teeth into'—

everything tastes great!

Whippet puppies are fairly aggressive chewers and only the hardest, strongest toys should be offered to them. Breeders advise owners to resist stuffed toys, because they can become de-stuffed in no time. The overly excited pup may ingest the stuffing, which is neither digestible nor nutritious.

Similarly, squeaky toys are quite popular, but must be avoided for the Whippet. 'De-squeaking' a toy is as instinctual to a Whippet as catching and killing a runaway hare. Perhaps a squeaky toy can be used as an aid in training, but not for free play. If a pup 'disembowels' one of these, the small plastic squeaker inside can be dangerous if swallowed.

TOYS, TOYS, TOYS!

With a big variety of dog toys available, and so many that look like they would be a lot of fun for a dog, be careful in your selection. It is amazing what a set of puppy teeth

can do to an innocent-looking toy, so, obviously, safety is a major consideration. Be sure to choose the most durable products that you can find. Hard nylon bones and toys are a safe bet, and many of them are offered in different scents and flavours that will be sure to capture your dog's attention. It is always fun to play a game of catch with your dog, and there are balls and flying discs that are specially made to withstand dog teeth.

Monitor the condition of all your pup's toys carefully and get rid of any that have been chewed to the point of becoming potentially

Pet shops usually carry a large assortment of dog toys. Never use toys or stuffed animals intended for humans as they are easily destructible and dangerous.

Pet shops usually have a wide selection of leads from which you can choose the colour, style and length that best suit your needs.

dangerous.

Be careful of natural bones, which have a tendency to splinter into sharp, dangerous pieces. Also be careful of rawhide, which can turn into pieces that are easy to swallow or into a mushy mess on your carpet.

LEAD

A nylon lead is probably the best option as it is the most resistant to puppy teeth should your pup take a liking to chewing on his lead. Of course, this is a habit that should be nipped in the bud, but if your pup likes to chew on his lead he has a very slim chance of being able to chew through the strong nylon. Nylon leads are also lightweight, which is good for a young Whippet who is just getting used to the idea of walking on a lead. For everyday walking and safety purposes, the nylon lead is a good choice. As your pup grows up and gets used to walking on the lead, you may want to purchase a flexible lead. These leads allow

you to extend the length to give the dog a broader area to explore or to shorten the length to keep the dog close to you. Of course there are special leads for training purposes, and specially made leather harnesses for the working Whippets, but these are not necessary for routine walks.

COLLAR

Your pup should get used to wearing a collar all the time since you will want to attach his ID tags to it. Plus, you have to attach the lead to something! A lightweight nylon collar is a good choice; make sure that it fits snugly enough so that the pup cannot wriggle out of it, but is loose enough so that it will not be uncomfortably tight around the pup's neck. You should be able to fit a finger between the pup and the collar. It may take some time for your pup to get used to wearing the collar, but soon he will not even notice that it is there. Never leave a heavy collar on the Whippet as it can injure the dog's sensitive skin around its neck.

FOOD AND WATER BOWLS

Your pup will need two bowls, one for food and one for water. You may want two sets of bowls, one for inside and one for outside, depending on where the dog will be fed and where he will be spending most

of his time. Stainless steel or sturdy plastic bowls are popular choices. Plastic bowls are more chewable. Dogs tend not to chew on the steel variety, which can be sterilised. It is important to buy sturdy bowls since anything is in danger of being chewed by puppy teeth and you do not want your dog to be constantly chewing apart his bowl (for his safety and for your purse!).

CLEANING SUPPLIES

Until a pup is house-trained you will be doing a lot of cleaning. Accidents will occur, which is okay in the beginning because the puppy does not know any better. All you can do

Stainless steel bowls are the most convenient for the Whippet. These feeding and watering bowls are virtually indestructible, rust-resistant and easily sanitised.

Purchase the best quality bowls that you can locate and they will last a dog's lifetime.

is be prepared to clean up any 'accidents.' Old rags, towels, newspapers and a safe disinfectant are good to have on hand.

BEYOND THE BASICS

The items previously discussed are the bare necessities. You will find out what else you need as you go along—grooming

Be a thoughtful, sanitary citizen and clean up after your dog.

PHOTO COURTESY OF MIKKI PET PRODUCTS.

The **BUCKLE COLLAR** is the standard collar used for everyday purpose. Be sure that you adjust the buckle on growing puppies. Check it every day. It can become too tight overnight! These collars can be made of leather or nylon. Attach your dog's identification tags to this collar.

The **HALTER** is for a trained dog that has to be restrained to prevent running away, chasing a cat and the like. Considered the most humane of all collars, it is frequently used on smaller dogs for which collars are not comfortable.

supplies, flea/tick protection, etc. These things will vary depending on your situation but it is important that you have everything you need to feed and make your Whippet comfortable in his first few days at home.

PUPPY-PROOFING

Aside from making sure that your Whippet will be comfortable in your home, you also have to make sure that your home is safe for your Whippet.

This means taking precautions that your pup will not get into anything he should not get into and that there is nothing within

his reach that may harm him should he sniff it, chew it, inspect it, etc. This probably seems obvious since, whilst you are primarily concerned with your pup's safety, at the same time you do not want your belongings to be ruined. Breakables should be placed out of reach if your dog is to have full run of the house. If he is to be limited to certain places within the house, keep any potentially dangerous items in the 'off-limits' areas. An electrical cable can pose a danger should the puppy decide to taste it—and who is going to convince a pup that it would not make a great chew toy? Cables should be fastened tightly against the wall. If your dog is going to spend time in a crate, make sure that there is nothing near his crate that he can reach if he sticks his curious little nose or paws through the openings. Just as you would with a child, keep all household cleaners and chemicals where the pup cannot get to them.

It is also important to make sure that the outside of your home is safe. Of course your puppy should never be unsupervised, but a pup let loose in the garden will want to run and explore, and he should be granted that freedom. Do not let a fence give you a false sense

TOXIC PLANTS

Many plants can be toxic to dogs. If you see your dog carrying a piece of vegetation in his mouth, approach him in a quiet, disinterested manner,

avoid eye contact, pet him and gradually remove the plant from his mouth. Alternatively, offer him a treat and maybe he'll drop the plant on his own accord. Be sure no toxic plants are growing in your own garden.

Puppies are amongst the most curious creatures in existence. Keep a watchful eye out whenever your Whippet is outside in the garden.

of security; you would be surprised how crafty (and persistent) a dog can be in working out how to dig under and squeeze his way through small holes, or to jump or climb over a fence. The remedy is to

PUPPY-PROOFING

Thoroughly puppy-proof your house before bringing your puppy home. Never use rodent poisons in any area accessible to the puppy. Avoid the

use of toilet cleaners. Most dogs are born with 'toilet sonar' and will take a drink if the lid is left open. Also keep the rubbish secured and out of reach. Scour your garage for potential puppy dangers. Remove weed killers, pesticides and antifreeze materials. Antifreeze is highly toxic and even a few drops can kill an adult dog. The sweet taste attracts the animal, who will quickly consume it from the floor or kerbside.

make the fence high enough so that it really is impossible for your dog to get over it (about 3 metres should suffice), and well embedded into the ground. Be sure to repair or secure any gaps in the fence. Check the fence periodically to ensure that it is in good shape and make repairs as needed; a very determined pup may return to the same spot to 'work on it' until he is able to get through.

FIRST TRIP TO THE VET
You have picked out your puppy, and your home and family are ready. Now all you have to do is collect your Whippet from the breeder and the fun begins, right? Well...not so fast. Something else you

need to prepare is your pup's first trip to the veterinary surgeon. Perhaps the breeder can recommend someone in the area that specialises in Whippets, or maybe you know some other Whippet owners who can suggest a good vet. Either way, you should have an appointment arranged for your pup before you pick him up and plan on taking him for an examination before bringing him home.

The pup's first visit will consist of an overall examination to make sure that the pup

CHEMICAL TOXINS

Scour your garage for potential puppy dangers. Remove weed killers, pesticides and antifreeze materials. Antifreeze is highly toxic and even a few drops can kill an adult dog. The sweet taste attracts the animal, who will quickly consume it from the floor or curbside.

does not have any problems that are not apparent to the eye. The veterinary surgeon will also set up a schedule for the pup's

Whippets should never be allowed freedom to roam in an unfenced area, no matter how well trained they are. Since a Whippet can easily outrun its owner, this practice must be strongly discouraged.

59

It is urgent that the young people in the household bond with the Whippet. After all, this is his new family and, being a pack animal, he needs a family for his psychological satisfaction.

vaccinations; the breeder will inform you of which ones the pup has already received and the vet can continue from there.

INTRODUCTION TO THE FAMILY

Everyone in the house will be excited about the puppy coming home and will want to pet him and play with him, but it is best to make the introductions low-key so as not to overwhelm the puppy. He is apprehensive already. It is the first time he has been separated from his

DID YOU KNOW?

Some experts in canine health advise that stress during a dog's early years of development can compromise and weaken his immune system and

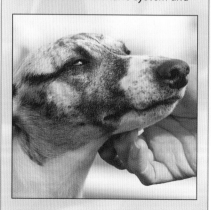

may trigger the potential for a shortened life expectancy. They emphasise the need for happy and stress-free growing-up years.

mother and the breeder, and the ride to your home is likely to be the first time he has been in a car. The last thing you want to do is smother him, as this will only frighten him further. This is not to say that human contact is not extremely necessary at this stage, because this is the time when a connection between the pup and his human family is formed. Gentle petting and soothing words should help console him, as well as just putting him down and letting him explore on his own (under your watchful eye, of course).

The pup may approach the

DID YOU KNOW?

The majority of problems that is commonly seen in young pups will disappear as your dog gets older. However, how you deal with problems when he is young will determine how he reacts to discipline as an adult dog. It is important to establish who is boss (hopefully it will be you!) right away when you are first bonding with your dog. This bond will set the tone for the rest of your life together.

New owners are replacing a mother's love. Most Whippet dams are dependable, responsible parents who bond closely with their pups.

family members or may busy himself with exploring for a while. Gradually, each person should spend some time with the pup, one at a time, crouching down to get as close to the pup's level as possible and letting him sniff his hands and petting him gently. He definitely needs human attention and he needs to be touched—this is how to form an

immediate bond. Just remember that the pup is experiencing a lot of things for the first time, at the same time. There are new people, new noises, new smells, and new things to investigate: so be gentle, be affectionate, and be as comforting as you can be.

YOUR PUP'S FIRST NIGHT

You have travelled home with your new charge safely in his crate. He's been to the vet for a thorough check-up, he's been weighed and his papers have been examined; perhaps he's even been vaccinated and wormed as well. He's met the family and he's licked the whole family, including the excited

children and the less-than-happy cat. He's explored his area, his new bed, the garden and anywhere else he's been permitted. He's eaten his first meal at home and relieved himself in the proper place. He's heard lots of new sounds, smelled new friends and seen more of the outside world than ever before.

That was just the first day! He's worn out and is ready for bed...or so you think!

It's puppy's first night and you are ready to say 'Good night'—keep in mind that this is puppy's first night ever to be sleeping alone. His dam and littermates are no longer at paw's length and he's a bit scared, cold and lonely. Be reassuring to your new family member. This is not the time to spoil him and give in to his inevitable whining.

Puppies whine. They whine to let the others know where they are and hopefully to get company out of it. Place your pup in his new bed or crate in his room and close the door. Mercifully, he may fall asleep without a peep. If the inevitable occurs, ignore the whining: he is fine. Be strong and keep his interest in mind. Do not allow your heart to become guilty and visit the pup. He will fall asleep.

Many breeders recommend placing a piece of bedding from his former home in his new bed

DID YOU KNOW?

It will take at least two weeks for your puppy to become accustomed to his new surroundings. Give him lots of love, attention, handling, frequent opportunities to relieve himself, a diet he likes to eat and a place he can call his own.

so that he recognises the scent of his littermates. Others still advise placing a hot water bottle in his bed for warmth. This latter may be a good idea provided the pup doesn't attempt to suckle—he'll get good and wet and may not fall asleep so fast.

Puppy's first night can be somewhat stressful for the pup and his new family. Remember that you are setting the tone of nighttime at your house. Unless you want to play with your pup every evening at 10 p.m., midnight and 2 a.m., don't initiate the habit. Your family will thank you, and so will your pup!

PREVENTING PUPPY PROBLEMS

SOCIALISATION

Now that you have done all of the preparatory work and have helped your pup get accustomed to his new home and family, it is about time for you to have some fun! Social-ising your Whippet pup gives you the opportunity to show off your new friend, and your pup gets to reap the benefits of being an adorable creature that people will want to pet and, in general, think is absolutely precious!

Besides getting to know his new family, your puppy should be exposed to other people, animals and situations, but of

TRAINING TIP

Training your puppy takes much patience and can be frustrating at times, but you should see results from your efforts. If you have a puppy that seems untrainable, take him to a trainer or behaviourist. The dog may have a personality problem that requires the help of a professional, or perhaps you need help in learning how to train your dog.

DO YOUR HOMEWORK

In order to know whether or not a puppy will fit into your lifestyle, you need to assess his personality. A good way to do this is to interact with his parents. Your pup inherits not only his appearance but also his personality and temperament from the sire and dam. If the parents are fearful or overly aggressive, these same traits may likely show up in your puppy.

course he must not come into close contact with dogs you don't know well until his course of injections is fully complete. This will help him become well adjusted as he grows up and less prone to being timid or fearful of the new things he will encounter. Your pup's socialisation began at the breeder's but now it is your responsibility to continue it. The socialisation he receives up until the age of 12 weeks is the most critical, as this is the

Puppies are very oral, often playing mouth games with their litter mates. These Whippet pups have been raised together from birth, yet seem to be still jostling for position.

time when he forms his impressions of the outside world. Be especially careful during the eight-to-ten-week period, also known as the fear period. The interaction he receives during this time should be gentle and reassuring. Lack of socialisation can manifest itself in fear and aggression as the dog grows up. He needs lots of human contact, affection, handling and exposure to other animals.

Once your pup has received his necessary vaccinations, feel free to take him out and about (on his lead, of course). Walk him around the neighbourhood, take him on your daily errands, let people pet him, let him meet other dogs and pets, etc. Puppies do not have to try to make friends; there will be no shortage of people who will want to introduce themselves. Just make sure that you carefully supervise each meeting. If the neighbourhood children want to say hello, for example, that is great—children and pups most often make great companions. Sometimes an excited child can unintentionally handle a pup too roughly, or an overzealous pup can playfully nip a little too hard. You want to make socialisation experiences positive ones. What a pup learns during this very formative stage will impact his attitude toward

SOCIALISATION

Thorough socialisation includes not only meeting new people but also being introduced to new experiences such as riding in the car, having his coat brushed, hearing the television, walking in

a crowd—the list is endless. The more your pup experiences, and the more positive the experiences are, the less of a shock and the less scary it will be for your pup to encounter new things.

future encounters. You want your dog to be comfortable around everyone. A pup that has a bad experience with a child may grow up to be a dog that is shy around or aggressive toward children.

CONSISTENCY IN TRAINING
Dogs, being pack animals, naturally need a leader, or else

65

they try to establish dominance in their packs. When you bring a dog into your family, the choice of who becomes the leader and who becomes the 'pack' is entirely up to you! Your pup's intuitive quest for dominance, coupled with the fact that it is nearly impossible to look at an adorable Whippet pup with his 'puppy-dog' eyes and his ears that seem to be going every which way, and not cave in, give the pup almost an unfair advantage in getting the upper hand! A pup will definitely test the waters to see what he can and cannot do. Do not give in to those pleading eyes—stand your ground when it comes to disciplining the pup and make sure that all family members do the same. It will only confuse the pup when Mother tells him to get off the sofa when he is used to sitting up there with Father to watch the nightly news. Avoid discrepancies by having all members of the household decide on the rules before the pup even comes home...and be consistent in enforcing them! Early training shapes the dog's personality, so you cannot be unclear in what you expect.

COMMON PUPPY PROBLEMS

The best way to prevent puppy problems is to be proactive in stopping an undesirable behaviour as soon as it starts. The old saying 'You can't teach an old dog new tricks' does not necessarily hold true, but it is true that it is much easier to discourage bad behaviour in a young developing pup than to wait until the pup's bad behaviour becomes the adult dog's bad habit. There are some problems that are especially prevalent in puppies as they develop.

NIPPING

As puppies start to teethe, they feel the need to sink their teeth into anything available...unfortunately that includes your fingers, arms, hair, and toes. You may find this behaviour cute for the first five seconds...until you feel just how sharp those puppy teeth are. This is something you want to discourage immediately and consistently with a firm 'No!' (or whatever number of firm 'No's' it takes for him to understand that you mean business). Then replace your finger with an appropriate chew toy. Whilst this behaviour is merely annoying when the dog is young, it can become dangerous as your Whippet's adult teeth grow in and his jaws develop, and he continues to think it is okay to gnaw on human appendages. Your Whippet does not mean any harm with a friendly nip, but he also does not know his own strength.

CRYING/WHINING

Your pup will often cry, whine, whimper, howl or make some type of commotion when he is left

CHEWING TIPS

Chewing goes hand in hand with nipping in the sense that a teething puppy is always looking for a way to soothe his aching gums. In this case, instead of chewing on you, he may have taken a liking to your favourite shoe or something else which he should not be chewing. Again, realise that this is a normal canine behaviour that does not need to be discouraged, only redirected. Your pup just needs to be taught what is acceptable to chew on and what is off limits. Consistently tell him NO when you catch him chewing on something forbidden and give him a chew toy. Conversely, praise him when you catch him chewing on something appropriate. In this way you are discouraging the inappropriate behaviour and reinforcing the desired behaviour. The puppy chewing should stop after his adult teeth have come in, but an adult dog continues to chew for various reasons—perhaps because he is bored, perhaps to relieve tension or perhaps he just likes to chew. That is why it is important to redirect his chewing when he is still young.

alone. This is basically his way of calling out for attention to make sure that you know he is there and that you have not forgotten about him. He feels insecure when he is left alone, when you are out of the house and he is in his crate or when you are in another part of the house and he cannot see you. The noise he is making is an expression of the anxiety he feels at being alone, so he needs to be taught that being alone is okay. You are not actually training the dog to stop making noise, you are training him to feel comfortable when he is alone and thus removing the need for him to make the noise. This is where the crate with cosy bedding comes in handy. You want to know that he is safe when you are not there to supervise, and you know that he will be safe in his crate rather than roaming freely about the house. In order for the pup to stay in his crate without making a fuss, he needs to be comfortable in his crate. On that note, it is extremely important that the crate is never used as a form of punishment, or the pup will have a negative association with the crate.

Accustom the pup to the crate in short, gradually increasing time intervals in which you put him in the crate, maybe with a treat, and stay in the room with him. If he cries or makes a fuss, do not go to him, but stay in his sight. Gradually he will realise that staying in his crate is all right without your help, and it will not be so traumatic for him when you are not around. You may want to leave the radio on softly when you leave the house; the sound of human voices may be comforting.

Opposite page: Puppies instinctively suck from their mother's teats almost immediately following birth. If they fail to do so, the breeder must hand feed them for a month or more. There is no better food for the puppy than its mother's milk, especially during the first month.

DIETARY AND FEEDING CONSIDERATIONS

Today the choices of food for your Whippet are many and varied. There are simply dozens of brands of food in all sorts of flavours and textures, ranging from puppy diets to those for seniors. There are even hypoallergenic and low-calorie diets available. Because your Whippet's food has a bearing on coat, health and temperament, it is essential that the most suitable diet is selected for a Whippet of his age. It is fair to say, however, that even dedicated owners can be somewhat perplexed by the enormous range of foods available. Only understanding what is best for your dog will help you reach a valued decision.

Dog foods are produced in three basic types: dried, semi-moist and tinned. Dried foods are useful for the cost-conscious for overall they tend to be less expensive than semi-moist or tinned. These contain the least fat and the most preservatives. In general tinned foods are made up of 60–70 percent water, whilst semi-moist ones often contain so much sugar that they are perhaps the least preferred by owners, even though their dogs seem to like them.

When selecting your dog's diet, three stages of development must be considered: the puppy stage, adult stage and the senior or veteran stage.

PUPPY STAGE

Puppies instinctively want to suck milk from their mother's teats and a normal puppy will exhibit this behaviour from just a few moments following birth. If puppies do not attempt to suckle within the first half-hour or so, they should be encouraged to do so by placing them on a nipple, having selected ones with plenty of milk. This early milk supply is important in providing colostrum to protect

DID YOU KNOW?

A good test for proper diet is the colour, odour and firmness of your dog's stool. A healthy dog usually produces three semi-hard stools per day. The stools should have no unpleasant odour. They should be the same colour from excretion to excretion.

the puppies during the first eight to ten weeks of their lives. Although a mother's milk is much better than any milk formula, despite there being some excellent ones available, if the puppies do not feed you will have to feed them yourself. For those with less experience, advice from a veterinary surgeon is important so that you feed not only the right quantity of milk but that of correct quality, fed at suitably frequent intervals, usually every two hours during the first few days of life.

Puppies should be allowed to nurse from their mothers for about the first six weeks, although from the third or fourth week you will have begun to introduce small portions of suitable solid food. Most breeders like to introduce alternate milk and meat meals initially, building up to weaning time.

By the time the puppies are

DID YOU KNOW?

You will probably start feeding your pup the same food that he has been getting from the breeder; the breeder should give you a few days' supply to start you off. Although you should not

give your pup too many treats, you will want to have puppy treats on hand for coaxing, training, rewards, etc. Be careful, though, as a small pup's calorie requirements are relatively low and a few treats can add up to almost a full day's worth of calories without the required nutrition.

seven or a maximum of eight weeks old, they should be fully weaned and fed solely on a proprietary puppy food, or a high-quality home prepared diet, as some Whippet owners prefer. However pork meat should not be included as it is overly rich and upsets the stomach of dogs. If preparing a special diet, it is most important that all bones are removed.

Selection of the most suitable, good-quality diet at this time is essential for a puppy's fastest growth rate is during the first year of life. Veterinary surgeons are usually able to offer advice in this regard. Although the frequency of meals will have been reduced over time, if using a proprietary feeding programme, change of diet will have been followed according to manufacturers' instructions.

Puppy and junior diets should be well balanced for the needs of your dog, so that except in certain circumstances additional vitamins, minerals and proteins will not be required.

ADULT DIETS

A dog is considered an adult when it has stopped growing, so in general the diet of a Whippet will have been changed to an adult one by 12 months of age, sometimes sooner depending on one's selection of diet. It is important that you select the food best suited to your dog's needs, for active dogs will require a different diet from those leading a very sedate life.

SENIOR DIETS

As dogs get older, their metabolism changes. The older dog usually exercises less, moves more slowly and sleeps more. This change in

WHAT ARE YOU FEEDING YOUR DOG?

1.3% Calcium
1.6% Fatty Acids
4.6% Crude Fibre
11% Moisture
14% Crude Fat
22% Crude Protein
45.5% ? ? ?

50%
40%
30%
20%
10%
0%

Read the label on your dog food. Many dog foods only advise what 50—55% of the contents are, leaving the other 45% in doubt.

As adults, Whippets tend to be more restful and calm, making fine companions for young and old alike. This young lady has a lovely rapport with her Whippet.

Sporting outlets like agility trials provide excellent means for Whippets to expend their energy. Whippets require more exercise than other dogs and welcome new challenges.

lifestyle and physiological performance requires a change in diet. Since these changes take place slowly, they might not be recognisable. What is easily recognisable is weight gain. By continuing to feed your dog an adult-maintenance diet when it is slowing down metabolically, your dog will gain weight. Obesity in an older dog compounds the health problems that already accompany old age.

As your dog gets older, few of his organs function up to par.

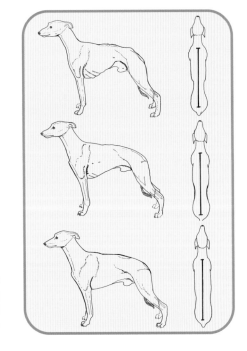

Illustrating profiles of dogs that are too thin (topmost); correct (centre); and too heavy (lower figure).

The kidneys slow down and the intestines become less efficient. These age-related factors are best handled with a change in diet and a change in feeding schedule to give smaller portions that are more easily digested.

There is no single best diet for every older dog. Whilst many dogs do well on light or senior diets, other dogs do better on puppy diets or other special premium diets such as lamb and rice. Be sensitive to your senior Whippet's diet and this will help control other problems that may arise with your old friend.

WATER
Just as your dog needs proper nutrition from his food, water is an essential 'nutrient' as well. Water keeps the dog's body properly hydrated and promotes normal function of the body's systems. During house-training it is necessary to keep an eye on how much water your Whippet is drinking, but once he is reliably trained he should have access to clean fresh water at all times. Make sure that the dog's water bowl is clean, and change the water often, making sure that water is always available for your dog, especially if you feed dried food.

EXERCISE
To retain fitness, vitality and muscle tone, Whippets need

FOOD PREFERENCE

Selecting the best dried dog food is difficult. There is no majority consensus amongst veterinary scientists as to the value of nutrient analyses (protein, fat, fibre, moisture, ash, cholesterol, minerals, etc.). All agree that feeding trials are what matters, but you also have to consider the individual dog. Its weight, age, activity and what pleases its taste, all must be considered. It is

probably best to take the advice of your veterinary surgeon. Every dog's dietary requirements vary, even during the lifetime of a particular dog.

If your dog is fed a good dried food, it does not require supplements of meat or vegetables. Dogs do appreciate a little variety in their diets so you may choose to stay with the same brand, but vary the flavour. Alternatively you may wish to add a little flavoured stock to give a difference to the taste.

73

DID YOU KNOW?

You must store your dried dog food carefully. Open packages of dog food quickly lose their vitamin value, usually within 90 days of being opened. Mould spores and vermin could also contaminate the food.

exercise and most breeders advocate a careful combination of roadwork on a lead and free run. Whippets are easy to lead walk, which enables owners with more than one Whippet to walk several together so that one's entire day does not have to be spent walking up and down the local lane, for each adult Whippet needs a couple of miles each day.

Whippets always seem to enjoy each other's company and will regularly play together, creating their own amusement and additional exercise.

Grooming gloves are a favourite with many Whippet owners. Gloves make grooming quick and easy, efficiently removing dead hair and dust from the coat.

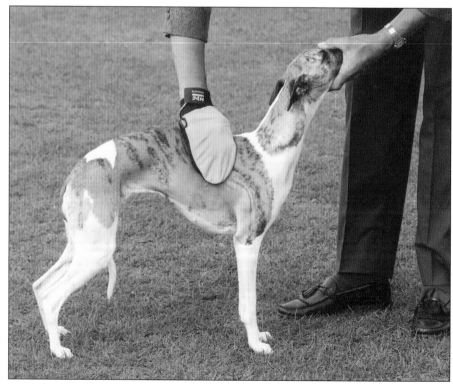

The short coat of a well-groomed Whippet will look sleek and shiny.

GROOMING EQUIPMENT

How much grooming equipment you purchase will depend on how much grooming you are going to do. Here are some basics:
- Natural bristle brush
- Slicker brush
- Metal comb
- Scissors
- Blaster
- Rubber mat
- Dog shampoo
- Spray hose attachment
- Ear cleaner
- Cotton wipes
- Towels
- Nail clippers
- Grooming glove

GROOMING

BRUSHING

With their short coats, Whippets require minimal grooming compared with many other breeds. Nonetheless, you should follow a routine grooming pattern. Only if attention is paid to coat, skin and nails, will they remain in tip-top condition so that your dog will not only look but also feel its best.

Short grooming sessions should be introduced from an early age. From the very beginning, a few minutes each day should be set aside, the duration building up slightly as the puppy matures. Your puppy

75

NO CHOCOLATE!

Use treats to bribe your dog into a desired behaviour. Try small pieces

of hard cheese or freeze-dried liver. Never offer chocolate as it has toxic qualities for dogs.

should be taught to stand calmly and quietly for grooming and for massage, both of which your dog will learn to enjoy.

ROUTINE GROOMING

Each owner has his own favourite way of grooming his dog, and hopefully other owners with whom you come into contact will freely pass on some

of their tips. Incidentally, Whippets benefit from massage for this helps to tone up the muscles.

A special rubber pad or grooming glove should be used to take out any dead hair. Various slightly differing gloves are available, some with very fine, short bristles attached to one side of the glove. A chamois leather, velvet or even a piece of silk can be used for finishing off. A useful grooming glove has chamois leather on one side and velvet on the other, which I find an admirable combination.

If a dog has dandruff problems a small amount of non-oily coat dressing can be applied, but this should be done at least a day before a show so that no residue is left in the coat.

BATHING AND DRYING

How frequently you decide to bath your Whippet will depend very much on personal preference, and the lifestyle led by your hound. Many Whippets are bathed occasionally just to freshen them up, whilst some people prefer to bath regularly before most shows, especially if their dogs are parti-coloured or have white in the coat.

When bathing my own dogs, I like them to stand on a non-slip mat in the bath, then I wet the coat thoroughly using a shower. It is imperative that the water temperature has previously been tested on your own hand. Use a good-quality shampoo designed especially for dogs. When this has been thoroughly rinsed out, if you wish you may apply a canine conditioner, then rinse again until the water runs clear. Many people like to use a baby shampoo on the head to avoid irritation to the eyes, and some like to plug the ears with cotton wool to avoid water getting inside them. Personally, I do neither of these, but taking care especially in that area, I have never encountered problems. Towel dry your dog whilst still in the bath and then help your Whippet carefully out of the bath. Undoubtedly your Whippet will want to shake—so be prepared!

If bathing during warm weather or in a heated home, drying this short-coated breed can be done more or less naturally. But never allow a dog to get cold after a bath, so make sure the environment is pleasantly warm and never allow your hound outdoors in cold weather until the coat is completely dry.

It is always worth remembering that if you really feel your dog's coat needs cleaning before a show but the

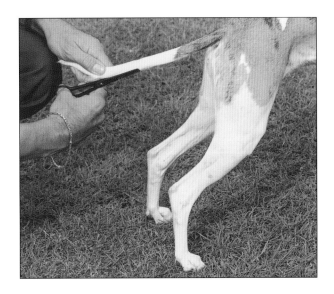

weather is too cold, or for the sake of convenience, a dry shampoo can be used. This will freshen the coat.

SCISSORING
Owners generally like to carefully tidy up stray hairs

Hairs on the Whippet's tail are often trimmed to give the tail a neater appearance.

DID YOU KNOW?

The use of human soap products like shampoo, bubble bath and hand soap can be damaging to a dog's coat and skin. Human products are too strong and remove the protective oils coating the dog's hair and skin (making him water-resistant). Use only shampoo made especially for dogs and you may like to use a medicated shampoo, which will always help to keep external parasites at bay.

This is the front paw of a Whippet. There are both light and dark nails.

under the tail and, if necessary, down the buttocks.

EAR CLEANING

Ears must always be kept clean. This can be done using a special liquid cleaner with a doggie cotton wipe. Many people use cotton buds, but this is not recommended since the Whippet's ears can be easily injured if an inexperienced owner delves too deeply.

Be on the lookout for any signs of infection or ear mite infestation. If your Whippet has been shaking his head or scratching at his ears frequently, this usually indicates a problem. If his ears have an unusual odour, this is a sure sign of mite infestation or infection, and a signal to have his ears checked by the veterinary surgeon.

NAIL CLIPPING

Your Whippet should be accustomed to having his nails trimmed at an early age, since it will be part of your maintenance routine throughout his life. Long

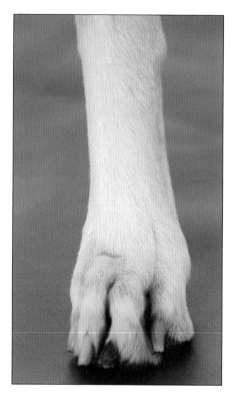

nails are uncomfortable for any dog and can scratch someone unintentionally. Also, a long nail has a better chance of ripping and bleeding, or causing the feet to spread. A Whippet's nails are very important and must be filed as well as clipped to get the very best finish.

Before you start cutting, make sure you can identify the 'quick' in each nail. The quick is a blood vessel that runs through the centre of each nail and grows rather close to the end. It will bleed if accidentally cut, which will be quite painful for the dog,

This is the back foot, showing well-trimmed nails in both light and dark colouration.

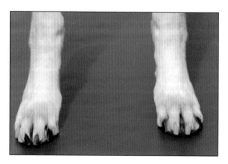

Nail Maintenance

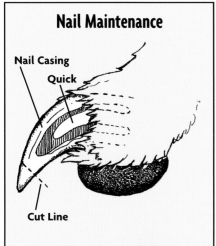

Nail Casing
Quick
Cut Line

Dark-Coloured Nails

With black or dark nails, where the quick is not easy to see, it's best to clip only the tip of the nail or to use a file.

Light-Coloured Nails

In light-coloured nails, clipping is much simpler because you can see the vein (or quick) that grows inside the casing.

as it contains nerve endings. Keep some type of clotting agent on hand, such as a styptic pencil or styptic powder (the type used for shaving). This will stop the bleeding quickly when applied to the end of the cut nail. Do not panic if this happens, just stop the bleeding and talk soothingly to your dog. Once he has calmed down, move on to the next nail. It is better to clip a little at a time, particularly with black-nailed dogs.

Hold your pup steady as you begin trimming his nails; you do not want him to make any sudden movements or run away. Talk to him soothingly and stroke him as you clip. Holding his foot in your hand, simply take off the end of each nail in one quick clip. You can purchase nail clippers that are specially made for dogs; you can probably find them wherever you buy pet or grooming supplies.

TRAVELLING WITH YOUR DOG

CAR TRAVEL

You should accustom your Whippet to riding in a car at an early age. You may or may not take him in the car often, but at the very least he will need to go to the vet and you do not want these trips to be traumatic for the dog or troublesome for you.

79

The safest way for a dog to ride in the car is in his crate. If he uses a crate in the house, you can use the same crate for travelling, or your car may be fitted with a specially designed dog-proof area, suitable for a Whippet in size.

Put the pup in the crate and see how he reacts. If he seems uneasy, you can have a passenger hold him on his lap whilst you drive. Another option is a specially made safety

TRAVEL TIP

When travelling, never let your dog off-lead in a strange area. Your dog

could run away out of fear or decide to chase a passing squirrel or cat or simply want to stretch his legs without restriction—you might never see your canine friend again.

TRAVEL TIP

If you are going on a long car trip with your dog, be sure the hotels are dog friendly. Many hotels do not accept dogs. Also take along some ice that can be thawed and offered to your dog if he becomes overheated. Most dogs like to lick ice.

harness for dogs, which straps the dog in much like a seat belt. Do not let the dog roam loose in the vehicle—this is very dangerous! If you should stop short, your dog can be thrown and injured. If the dog starts climbing on you and pestering you whilst you are driving, you will not be able to concentrate on the road. It is an unsafe situation for everyone—human and canine.

For long trips, be prepared to stop to let the dog relieve himself. Bring along whatever you need to clean up after him. You should take along some paper kitchen towels and perhaps some old towelling for use should he have an accident in the car or suffer from travel sickness.

AIR TRAVEL
With the advent of the PETS Passport Scheme air travel with dogs is becoming more popular.

The dog will be required to travel in a fibreglass crate and you should always check in advance with the airline regarding specific requirements. To help the dog be at ease, put one of his favourite toys in the crate with him. Do not feed the dog for at least six hours before the trip to minimise his need to relieve himself. However, certain regulations specify that water must always be made available to the dog in the crate.

Make sure your dog is properly identified and that your contact information appears on his ID tags and on his crate. Animals travel in a different area of the plane than human passengers so every rule must be strictly adhered to so as to prevent the risk of getting separated from your dog.

BOARDING

So you want to take a family holiday—and you want to include *all* members of the family. You would probably make arrangements for accommodations ahead of time anyway, but this is especially important when travelling with a dog. You do not want to make an overnight stop at the only place around for miles and find out that they do not allow dogs. Also, you do not want to reserve a place for your family without confirming that you are travel-

ling with a dog because if it is against their policy you may not have a place to stay.

Alternatively, if you are travelling and choose not to bring your Whippet, you will have to make arrangements for him whilst you are away. Some options are to take him to a neighbour's house to stay whilst you are gone, to have a trusted neighbour stop by often or stay at your house, or bring your dog to a reputable boarding kennel. If you choose to board him at a kennel, you should visit in

TRAVEL TIP

For international travel you will have to make arrangements well in advance (perhaps months), as countries' regulations pertaining to bringing in animals differ. There may be special health certificates and/or vaccinations that your dog will need before taking the trip; sometimes this has to be done within a certain time frame. In rabies-free countries, you will need to bring proof of the dog's rabies vaccination and there may be a quarantine period upon arrival.

advance to see the facilities provided, how clean they are and where the dogs are kept. Talk to some of the employees and see how they treat the dogs—do they spend time with the dogs, play with them, exercise them, etc.? Also find out the kennel's policy on vaccinations and what they require. This is for all of the dogs' safety, since when dogs are kept together, there is a greater risk of diseases being passed from dog to dog.

Select a boarding kennel that is clean, well staffed with friendly dog people and spacious enough to provide the dogs with runs for regular exercise.

IDENTIFICATION

Your Whippet is your valued companion and friend. That is why you always keep a close

eye on him and you have made sure that he cannot escape from the garden or wriggle out of his collar and run away from you. However, accidents can happen and there may come a time when your dog unexpectedly gets separated from you. If this unfortunate event should occur, the first thing on your mind will be finding him. Proper identification, including an ID tag, a tattoo, and possibly a microchip, will increase the chances of his being returned to you safely and quickly.

Be sure your Whippet's identification tag is current, complete and securely fastened to his collar.

Don't risk your Whippet's safety. A tattoo on his thigh is insurance against dog theft. This photo has been retouched for clarity.

DID YOU KNOW?

If you start with a normal, healthy dog and give him time, patience and some carefully executed lessons, you will reap the rewards of that training for the life of the dog. And what a

life it will be! The two of you will find immeasurable pleasure in the companionship you have built together with love, respect and understanding.

Living with an untrained dog is a lot like owning a piano that you do not know how to play—it is a nice object to look at but it does not do much more than that to bring you pleasure. Now try taking piano lessons and suddenly the piano comes alive and brings forth magical sounds and rhythms that set your heart singing and your body swaying.

The same is true with your Whippet. Any dog is a big responsibility and if not trained sensibly may develop unacceptable behaviour that annoys you or could even cause family friction.

To train your Whippet, you may like to enrol in an obedience class. Teach him good manners as you learn how and why he behaves the way he does. Find out how to communicate with your dog and how to recognise and understand his communications with you. Suddenly the dog takes on a new role in your life—he is clever, interesting, well behaved and fun to be with. He demonstrates his bond of devotion to you daily. In other words, your Whippet does wonders for your ego because he constantly reminds you that you are not only his leader, you are his hero!

Those involved with teaching dog obedience and counselling owners about their dogs' behaviour have discovered some interesting facts about dog ownership. For example, training dogs when they are puppies results in the highest rate of success in developing well-mannered and well-adjusted adult dogs. Training an older dog, from six months to six years of age, can produce almost equal results providing that the owner accepts the dog's slower rate of learning capability and is willing to work patiently to help the dog succeed at developing to his fullest potential. Unfortunately, many owners of untrained adult dogs lack the patience factor, so they do not persist until their dogs are successful at learning particular behaviours.

Training a puppy, aged 10 to 16 weeks (20 weeks at the most) is like working with a dry sponge in a pool of water. The pup soaks up whatever you show him and constantly looks for more things to do and learn. At this early age, his body is not yet producing hormones, and therein lies the reason for such a high rate of success. Without hormones, he is focused on his owners and not particularly interested in investigating other places, dogs, people, etc. You are his leader: his provider of food, water, shelter and security. He latches onto you and wants to stay close. He will usually follow you from room to room,

OBEDIENCE SCHOOL

Taking your dog to an obedience school may be the best investment in time and money you can ever make. You will enjoy the benefits for the lifetime of your dog and you will have the opportunity to meet people with your similar expectations for companion dogs.

Ch Silkstone Jewel in the Crown demonstrates the virtues of good training (and good breeding). This Whippet is a Best in Show winner, owned by Frank and Lee Pieterse.

TRAINING TIP

Training a dog is a life experience. Many parents admit that much of what they know about raising children they learned from caring for their dogs. Dogs respond to love,

fairness and guidance, just as children do. Become a good dog owner and you may become an even better parent.

happy to greet the person as well. If, however, you are hesitant, even anxious, about the approach of a stranger, he will respond accordingly.

Once the puppy begins to produce hormones, his natural curiosity emerges and he begins to investigate the world around him. It is at this time when you may notice that the untrained dog begins to wander away from

will not let you out of his sight when you are outdoors with him, and will respond in like manner to the people and animals you encounter. If you greet a friend warmly, he will be

you and even ignore your commands to stay close. When this behaviour becomes a problem, the owner has two choices: get rid of the dog or train him. It is strongly urged that you choose the latter option.

There are usually classes within a reasonable distance from the owner's home, but you also do a lot to train your dog yourself. Sometimes there are

DID YOU KNOW?

To a dog's way of thinking, your hands are like his mouth in terms of a defence mechanism. If you squeeze

him too tightly, he might just bite you because that would be his normal response. This is not aggressive biting and, although all biting should be discouraged, you need the discipline in learning how to handle your dog.

classes available but the tuition is too costly. Whatever the circumstances, the solution to the problem of lack of lesson availability lies within the pages of this book.

Dog training is a matter of dedication, repetition and communication. If your Whippet will look you in the eye, he is willing to learn.

87

DID YOU KNOW?

Dogs are the most honourable animals in existence. They consider another species (humans) as their own. They interface with you. You are their leader. Puppies perceive

children to be on their level; their actions around small children are different from their behaviour around their adult masters.

This chapter is devoted to helping you train your Whippet at home. If the recommended procedures are followed faithfully, you may expect positive results that will prove rewarding to both you and your dog.

Whether your new charge is a puppy or a mature adult, the methods of teaching and the techniques we use in training basic behaviours are the same. After all, no dog, whether puppy or adult, likes harsh or inhumane methods. All creatures, however, respond favourably to gentle motivational methods and sincere praise and encouragement. Now let us get started.

HOUSE-TRAINING
You can train a puppy to relieve itself wherever you choose, but this must be somewhere suitable. You should bear in mind from the outset that when your puppy is old enough to go out in public places, any canine deposits must be removed at once. You will always have to carry with you a small plastic bag or 'poop-scoop.'

Outdoor training includes such surfaces as grass, mud, soil or earth and cement. Indoor training usually means training your dog to newspaper.

When deciding on the surface and location that you will want your Whippet to use, be sure it is going to be permanent. Training your dog to grass and then changing your mind two months later is extremely difficult for both dog and owner.

Next, choose the command you will use each and every time you want your puppy to void. 'Be quick,' 'Hurry up' and 'Toilet' are examples of commands commonly used by dog owners.

Get in the habit of giving the puppy your chosen relief command before you take him out. That way, when he becomes an adult, you will be able to determine if he wants to go out when you ask him. A confirmation will be signs of interest, wagging his tail, watching you intently, going to the door, etc.

PUPPY'S NEEDS

Puppy needs to relieve himself after play periods, after each meal, after he has been sleeping and any time he indicates that he is looking for a place to urinate or defecate.

The urinary and intestinal tract muscles of very young puppies are not fully developed. Therefore, like human babies, puppies need to relieve themselves frequently.

Take your puppy out often—every hour for an eight-week-old, for example, and always immediately after sleeping and eating. The older the puppy, the less often he will need to relieve himself. Finally, as a mature healthy adult, he will require only three to five relief trips per day.

HOUSE-TRAINING TIP

Most of all, be consistent. Always take your dog to the same location, always use the same command, and always have him on lead when he is in his relief area, unless a fenced-in garden is available.

By following the Success Method, your puppy will be completely house-trained by the time his muscle and brain development reach maturity. Keep in mind that small breeds usually mature faster than large breeds, but all puppies should be trained by six months of age.

HOUSING

Since the types of housing and control you provide for your puppy have a direct relationship on the success of house-training, we consider the various aspects of both before we begin training.

Bringing a new puppy home and turning him loose in your house can be compared to turning a child loose in a sports

DID YOU KNOW?

HOW MANY TIMES A DAY?

AGE	RELIEF TRIPS
To 14 weeks	10
14–22 weeks	8
22–32 weeks	6
Adulthood	4
(dog stops growing)	

These are estimates, of course, but they are a guide to the MINIMUM opportunities a dog should have each day to relieve itself.

watching you whilst you are doing things and smelling you nearby are all positive reinforcers that he is now a member of your pack. Usually a family room, the kitchen or a nearby adjoining breakfast area is ideal for providing safety and security for both puppy and owner.

Within that room there should be a smaller area which the puppy can call his own. An alcove, a wire or fibreglass dog crate or a fenced (not boarded!) corner from which he can view the activities of his new family will be fine. The size of the area or crate is the key factor here. The area must be large enough for the puppy to lie down and stretch out as well as stand up without rubbing his head on the top, yet small enough so that he cannot relieve himself at one end and sleep at the other without coming into contact with his droppings until fully trained to relieve himself outside.

Dogs are, by nature, clean animals and will not remain close to their relief areas unless forced to do so. In those cases, they then become dirty dogs and usually remain that way for life.

The designated area should be lined with clean bedding and a toy. Water must always be available, in a non-spill container.

arena and telling the child that the place is all his! The sheer enormity of the place would be too much for him to handle.

Instead, offer the puppy clearly defined areas where he can play, sleep, eat and live. A room of the house where the family gathers is the most obvious choice. Puppies are social animals and need to feel a part of the pack right from the start. Hearing your voice,

Whippets can be a tad clannish and keep secrets from their human pack members.

CONTROL

By control, we mean helping the puppy to create a lifestyle pattern that will be compatible to that of his human pack (YOU!). Just as we guide little children to learn our way of life, we must show the puppy when it is time to play, eat, sleep, exercise and even entertain himself.

Your puppy should always sleep in his crate. He should also learn that, during times of household confusion and excessive human activity such as at breakfast when family members are preparing for the day, he can play by himself in relative safety and comfort in his designated area. Each time you leave the puppy alone, he should understand exactly where he is to stay. Puppies are chewers. They cannot tell the difference between lamp cables, television wires, shoes, table legs, etc. Chewing into a television wire, for example, can be fatal to the puppy whilst a shorted wire can start a fire in the house.

PRACTICE MAKES PERFECT

- Have training lessons with your dog every day in several short segments—three to five times a day for a few minutes at a time is ideal.
- Do not have long practice sessions. The dog will become easily bored.
- Never practise when you are tired, ill,

worried or in an otherwise negative mood. This will transmit to the dog and may have an adverse effect on its performance.

Think fun, short and above all POSITIVE! End each session on a high note, rather than a failed exercise, and make sure to give a lot of praise. Enjoy the training and help your dog enjoy it, too.

If the puppy chews the arm of the chair when he is alone, you will probably discipline him angrily when you get home. Thus, he makes the association that your coming home means he is going to be punished. (He will not remember chewing the chair and is incapable of making the association of the discipline with his naughty deed.)

Other times of excitement, such as family parties, etc., can be fun for the puppy providing he can view the activities from the security of his designated area. He is not underfoot and he is not being fed all sorts of titbits that will probably cause him stomach distress, yet he still feels a part of the fun.

SCHEDULE

A puppy should be taken to his relief area each time he is released from his designated area, after meals, after a play session and when he first awakens in the morning (at age eight weeks, this can mean 5 a.m.!). The puppy will indicate that he's ready 'to go' by circling or sniffing busily—do not misinterpret these signs. For a puppy less than ten weeks of age, a routine of taking him out every hour is necessary. As the puppy grows, he will be able to wait for longer periods of time.

Keep trips to his relief area short. Stay no more than five or six minutes and then return to the house. If he goes during that time, praise him lavishly and take him indoors immediately. If he does not, but he has an accident when you go back indoors, pick him up immediately, say 'No! No!' and return to his relief area. Wait a few minutes, then return to the house again. Never hit a puppy or rub his face in urine or excrement when he has an accident!

Once indoors, put the puppy in his crate until you have had time to clean up his accident. Then release him to the family area and watch him more closely than before. Chances are, his accident was a result of your not picking up his signal or waiting too long before offering him the opportunity to relieve himself. Never hold a grudge against the puppy for accidents.

Let the puppy learn that going outdoors means it is time to relieve himself, not play. Once trained, he will be able to play indoors and out and still differentiate between the times for play versus the times for relief.

Help him develop regular hours for naps, being alone, playing by himself and just resting, all in his crate. Encourage him to entertain himself whilst you are busy

DID YOU KNOW?

The puppy should also have regular play and exercise sessions when he is with you or a family member. Exercise for a very young puppy can consist of a short walk around the house or garden. Playing can include fetching games with a large ball or a special raggy. (All puppies teethe and need soft things upon which to chew.) Remember to restrict play periods to indoors within his living area (the family room, for example) until he is completely house-trained.

93

CANINE DEVELOPMENT SCHEDULE

It is important to understand how and at what age a puppy develops into adulthood. If you are a puppy owner, consult the following Canine Development Schedule to determine the stage of development your puppy is currently experiencing. This knowledge will help you as you work with the puppy in the weeks and months ahead.

Period	Age	Characteristics
FIRST TO THIRD	BIRTH TO SEVEN WEEKS	Puppy needs food, sleep and warmth, and responds to simple and gentle touching. Needs mother for security and disciplining. Needs littermates for learning and interacting with other dogs. Pup learns to function within a pack and learns pack order of dominance. Begin socialising with adults and children for short periods. Begins to become aware of its environment.
FOURTH	EIGHT TO TWELVE WEEKS	Brain is fully developed. Needs socialising with outside world. Remove from mother and littermates. Needs to change from canine pack to human pack. Human dominance necessary. Fear period occurs between 8 and 16 weeks. Avoid fright and pain.
FIFTH	THIRTEEN TO SIXTEEN WEEKS	Training and formal obedience should begin. Less association with other dogs, more with people, places, situations. Period will pass easily if you remember this is pup's change-to-adolescence time. Be firm and fair. Flight instinct prominent. Permissiveness and over-disciplining can do permanent damage. Praise for good behaviour.
JUVENILE	FOUR TO EIGHT MONTHS	Another fear period about 7 to 8 months of age. It passes quickly, but be cautious of fright and pain. Sexual maturity reached. Dominant traits established. Dog should understand sit, down, come and stay by now.

NOTE: THESE ARE APPROXIMATE TIME FRAMES. ALLOW FOR INDIVIDUAL DIFFERENCES IN PUPPIES.

with your activities. Let him learn that having you near is comforting, but it is not your main purpose in life to provide him with undivided attention.

Each time you put a puppy in his own area, use the same command, whatever suits best. Soon, he will run to his crate or special area when he hears you say those words.

Crate training provides safety for you, the puppy and the home. It also provides the puppy with a feeling of security, and that helps the puppy

SUCCESS METHOD

Success that comes by luck is usually short lived. Success that comes by well-thought-out proven methods is often more easily achieved and permanent. This is the Success Method. It is designed to give you, the puppy owner, a simple yet proven way to help your puppy develop clean living habits and a feeling of security in his new environment.

THE SUCCESS METHOD

1 Tell the puppy 'Crate time!' and place him in the crate with a small treat (a piece of cheese or half of a biscuit). Let him stay in the crate for five minutes while you are in the same room. Then release him and praise lavishly. Never release him when he is fussing. Wait until he is quiet before you let him out.

2 Repeat Step 1 several times a day.

3 The next day, place the puppy in the crate as before. Let him stay there for ten minutes. Do this several times.

4 Continue building time in five-minute increments until the puppy

stays in his crate for 30 minutes with you in the room. Always take him to his relief area after prolonged periods in his crate.

5 Now go back to Step 1 and let the puppy stay in his crate for five minutes, this time while you are out of the room.

6 Once again, build crate time in five-minute increments with you out of the room. When the puppy will stay willingly in his crate (he may even fall asleep!) for 30 minutes with you out of the room, he will be ready to stay in it for several hours at a time.

6 Steps to Successful Crate Training

HOUSE-TRAINING TIP

Do not carry your dog to his toilet area. Lead him there on a lead or, better yet, encourage him to follow

you to the spot. If you start carrying him to his spot, you might end up doing this routine forever and your dog will have the satisfaction of having trained YOU.

achieve self-confidence and clean habits.

Remember that one of the primary ingredients in house-training your puppy is control. Regardless of your lifestyle, there will always be occasions when you will need to have a place where your dog can stay and be happy and safe. Crate training is the answer for now and in the future.

In conclusion, a few key elements are really all you need for a successful house-training method—consistency, frequency, praise, control and supervision. By following these procedures with a normal, healthy puppy, you and the puppy will soon be past the stage of 'accidents' and ready to move on to a full and rewarding life together.

ROLES OF DISCIPLINE, REWARD AND PUNISHMENT

Discipline, training one to act in accordance with rules, brings order to life. It is as simple as that. Without discipline, particularly in a group society, chaos reigns supreme and the group will eventually perish. Humans and canines are social animals and need some form of discipline in order to function effectively. They must procure food, protect their home base and their young and reproduce to keep the species going.

If there were no discipline in the lives of social animals, they would eventually die from starvation and/or predation by other stronger animals.

In the case of domestic canines, dogs need discipline in their lives in order to understand how their pack (you and other family members) functions and how they must act in order to survive.

A large humane society in a highly populated area surveyed dog owners regarding their satisfaction with their relationships with their dogs. People who had trained their dogs were 75% more satisfied with their pets than those who had never trained their dogs.

Dr Edward Thorndike, a psychologist, established *Thorndike's Theory of Learning,* which states that a behaviour that results in a pleasant event tends to be repeated. A behaviour that results in an unpleasant event tends not to be repeated. It is this theory on which training methods are based today. For example, if you manipulate a dog to perform a specific behaviour and reward him for doing it, he is likely to do it again because he enjoyed the end result.

Occasionally, punishment, a penalty inflicted for an offence, is necessary. The best type of punishment often comes from an outside source. For example, a child is told not to touch the stove because he may get burned. He disobeys and touches the stove. In doing so, he receives a burn. From that time on, he respects the heat of the stove and avoids contact with it. Therefore, a behaviour

that results in an unpleasant event tends not to be repeated.

A good example of a dog learning the hard way is the dog who chases the house cat. He is told many times to leave the cat alone, yet he persists in teasing the cat. Then, one day he begins chasing the cat but the cat turns and swipes a claw across the dog's face, leaving him with a painful gash on his nose. The final result is that the dog stops chasing the cat.

DID YOU KNOW?

If you have other pets in the home and/or interact often with the pets of friends and other family

members, your pup will respond to those pets in much the same manner as you do. It is only when you show fear of or resentment toward another animal that he will act fearful or unfriendly.

must be one with which you are easily able to work, not too heavy for the dog and perfectly safe.

TREATS
Have a bag of treats on hand. Something nutritious and easy to swallow works best. Use a soft treat, a chunk of cheese or a piece of cooked chicken rather than a dry biscuit. By the time the dog has finished chewing a dry treat, he will forget why he is being rewarded in the first place! Using food rewards will not teach a dog to beg at the table—the only way to teach a dog to beg at the table is to give him food from the table. In training, rewarding the dog with a food treat will help him associate praise and the treats with learning new behaviours that obviously please his owner.

Once trained, Whippets are consistent and reliable, which are ideal traits for dogs pursuing a show career.

The use of treats is an accepted, effective practice in dog training. The dog is rewarded when it successfully performs an obedience command.

TRAINING EQUIPMENT

COLLAR AND LEAD
For a Whippet the collar and lead that you use for training

DID YOU KNOW?

Dogs will do anything for your attention. If you reward the dog when he is calm and resting, you will develop a well-mannered dog. If, on the other hand, you greet your dog excitedly and encourage him to wrestle and roughhouse with you, the dog will greet you the same way and you will have a hyper dog on your hands.

TRAINING BEGINS: ASK THE DOG A QUESTION

In order to teach your dog anything, you must first get his attention. After all, he cannot learn anything if he is looking away from you with his mind on something else.

To get his attention, ask him, 'School?' and immediately walk over to him and give him a treat as you tell him 'Good dog.' Wait a minute or two and repeat the routine, this time with a treat in your hand as you approach within a foot of the dog. Do not go directly to him, but stop about a foot short of him and hold out the treat as you ask, 'School?' He will see you approaching with a treat in your hand and most likely begin walking toward you. As you meet, give him the treat and praise again.

The third time, ask the question, have a treat in your hand and walk only a short distance toward the dog so that he must walk almost all the way to you. As he reaches you, give him the treat and praise again.

By this time, the dog will probably be getting the idea that if he pays attention to you, especially when you ask that question, it will pay off in treats and enjoyable activities for him. In other words, he learns that 'School' means doing things with you that result in treats and positive attention for him.

Remember that the dog does not understand your verbal language, he only recognises sounds. Your question translates to a series of sounds for him, and those sounds become the signal to go to you and pay attention; if he does, he will get to interact with you plus receive treats and praise.

Training your Whippet to sit upon command is only a first step in voice commands.

THE BASIC COMMANDS

TEACHING SIT

Now that you have the dog's attention, attach his lead and hold it in your left hand and a food treat in your right. Place your food hand at the dog's nose and let him lick the treat but not take it from you. Say 'Sit' and slowly raise your food hand from in front of the dog's nose

99

up over his head so that he is looking at the ceiling. As he bends his head upward, he will have to bend his knees to maintain his balance. As he bends his knees, he will assume a sit position. At that point, release the food treat and praise

lavishly with comments such as 'Good dog! Good sit!', etc. Remember to always praise enthusiastically, because dogs relish verbal praise from their owners and feel so proud of themselves whenever they accomplish a behaviour.

You will not use food forever in getting the dog to obey your commands. Food is only used to teach new behaviours, and once the dog knows what you want when you give a specific command, you will wean him off the food treats but still maintain the verbal praise. After all, you will always have your voice with you, and there will be many times when you have no food rewards but expect the dog to obey.

TEACHING DOWN

Teaching the down exercise is easy when you understand how the dog perceives the down position, and it is very difficult when you do not. Dogs perceive the down position as a submissive one, therefore teaching the down exercise using a forceful method can sometimes make the dog develop such a fear of the down that he either runs away when you say 'Down' or he attempts to snap at the person who tries to force him down.

Have the dog sit close alongside your left leg, facing in the same direction as you are. Hold the lead in your left hand and a food treat in your right. Now place your left hand lightly on the top of the dog's shoulders where they meet above the spinal cord. Do not push down on the dog's shoulders; simply rest your left hand there so you can guide the dog to lie down close to your left leg rather than to swing away from your side when he drops.

Now place the food hand at the dog's nose, say 'Down' very softly (almost a whisper), and slowly lower the food hand to the dog's front feet. When the food hand reaches the floor, begin moving it forward along the floor in front of the dog. Keep talking softly to the dog, saying things like, 'Do you want this treat? You can do this, good dog.' Your reassuring tone of voice will help calm the dog as he tries to follow the food hand in order to get the treat.

When the dog's elbows touch the floor, release the food and praise softly. Try to get the dog to maintain that down position for several seconds before you let him sit up again. The goal here is to get the dog to settle down and not feel threatened in the down position.

TEACHING STAY

It is easy to teach the dog to stay in either a sit or a down position. Again, we use food and praise during the teaching process as we help the dog to understand exactly what it is that we are expecting him to do.

To teach the sit/stay, start with the dog sitting on your left side as before and hold the lead in your left hand. Have a food treat in your right hand and place your food hand at the dog's nose. Say 'Stay' and step out on your right foot to stand directly in

DID YOU KNOW?

A dog in jeopardy never lies down. He stays alert on his feet because instinct tells him that he may have to run away or fight for his survival. Therefore, if a dog feels threatened or anxious, he will not lie down. Consequently, it is important to have the dog calm and relaxed as he learns the down exercise.

front of the dog, toe to toe, as he licks and nibbles the treat. Be sure to keep his head facing upward to maintain the sit position. Count to five and then swing around to stand next to the dog again with him on your left. As soon as you get back to the original position, release the food and praise lavishly.

DID YOU KNOW?

Dogs do not understand our language. They can be trained to react to a certain sound, at a certain volume. If you say 'No, Oliver' in a very soft pleasant voice it will not have the same meaning as 'No, Oliver!!' when you shout it as loud as you can. You should never use the dog's name during a reprimand, just

the command NO!! Since dogs don't understand words, comics often use dogs trained with opposite meanings. Thus, when the comic commands his dog to SIT the dog will stand up, and vice versa.

To teach the down/stay, do the down as previously described. As soon as the dog lies down, say 'Stay' and step out on your right foot just as you did in the sit/stay. Count to five and then return to stand beside the dog with him on your left

side. Release the treat and praise as always.

Within a week or ten days, you can begin to add a bit of distance between you and your dog when you leave him. When you do, use your left hand open with the palm facing the dog as a stay signal, much the same as the hand signal a constable uses to stop traffic at an intersection. Hold the food treat in your right hand as before, but this time the food is not touching the dog's nose. He will watch the food hand and quickly learn that he is going to get that treat as soon as you return to his side.

When you can stand 1 metre away from your dog for 30 seconds, you can then begin building time and distance in both stays. Eventually, the dog can be expected to remain in the stay position for prolonged periods of time until you return to him or call him to you. Always praise lavishly when he stays.

TEACHING COME

If you make teaching 'Come' a positive experience, you should never have a 'student' that does not love the game or that fails to come when called. The secret, it seems, is never to teach the word 'Come.'

At times when an owner most wants his dog to come when called, the owner is likely upset or anxious and he allows these feelings to come through in the tone of his voice when he calls his dog. Hearing that desperation in his owner's voice, the dog fears the results of going to him and therefore either disobeys outright or runs in the opposite direction. The secret, therefore, is to teach the dog a game and, when you want him to come to you, simply play the game. It is practically a no-fail solution!

To begin, have several members of your family take a few food treats and each go into a different room in the house. Take turns calling the dog, and each person should celebrate the dog's

TRAINING TIP

Never call your dog to come to you for a correction or scold him when he reaches you. That is the quickest way to turn a 'Come' command into 'Go away fast!' Dogs think only in the present tense, and your dog will connect the scolding with coming to you, not with the misbehaviour of a few moments earlier.

finding him with a treat and lots of happy praise. When a person calls the dog, he is actually inviting the dog to find him and get a treat as a reward for 'winning.'

Your Whippet(s) should come running when called. Teaching come should be an enjoyable time for you and your Whippet.

TRAINING TIP

When calling the dog, do not say 'Come.' Say things like, 'Rover, where are you? See if you can find me! I have a biscuit for you!' Keep up a constant line of chatter with coaxing sounds and frequent questions such as, 'Where are you?' The dog will learn to follow the sound of your voice to locate you and receive his reward.

A few turns of the 'Where are you?' game and the dog will understand that everyone is playing the game and that each person has a big celebration awaiting his success at locating them. Once he learns to love the game, simply calling out 'Where are you?' will bring him running from wherever he is when he hears that all-important question.

The come command is recognised as one of the most important things to teach a dog, but there are trainers who work with thousands of dogs and never teach the actual word 'Come.' Yet these dogs will race to respond to a person who uses the dog's name followed by 'Where are you?' For example, a woman has a 12-year-old companion dog who went blind, but who never fails to locate her owner when asked, 'Where are you?'

Children particularly love to play this game with their dogs. Children can hide in smaller places like a shower or bath, behind a bed or under a table. The dog needs to work a little bit harder to find these hiding places, but when he does he loves to celebrate with a treat and a tussle with a favourite youngster.

TEACHING HEEL

Heeling means that the dog walks beside the owner without pulling. It takes time and patience on the owner's part to succeed at teaching the dog that he (the owner) will not proceed unless the dog is walking calmly beside him. Pulling out ahead on the lead is definitely not acceptable.

Begin with holding the lead in your left hand as the dog sits beside your left leg. Move the loop end of the lead to your right hand but keep your left hand short on the lead so it keeps the

TRAINING TIP

If you begin teaching the heel by taking long walks and letting the dog pull you along, he misinterprets this action as an acceptable form of taking a walk. When you pull back on the lead to counteract his pulling, he reads that tug as a signal to pull even harder!

TRAINING TIP

Teach your dog to HEEL in an enclosed area. Once you think the dog will obey reliably and you want to attempt advanced obedience exercises such as off-lead heeling, test him in a fenced-in area so he cannot run away.

dog in close next to you.

Say 'Heel' and step forward on your left foot. Keep the dog close to you and take three steps. Stop and have the dog sit next to you in what we now call the 'heel position.' Praise verbally, but do not touch the dog. Hesitate a moment and begin again with 'Heel,' taking three steps and stopping, at which point the dog is told to sit again.

Your goal here is to have the dog walk those three steps without pulling on the lead. When he will walk calmly

TRAINING TIP

Dogs are sensitive to their master's moods and emotions. Use your voice wisely when communicating with your dog. Never raise your voice at your dog unless you are angry and trying to correct him. 'Barking' at your dog can become as meaningless as 'dogspeak' is to you. Think before you bark!

beside you for three steps without pulling, increase the number of steps you take to five. When he will walk politely beside you whilst you take five steps, you can increase the length of your walk to ten steps.

All training should take place in a safe location where there are no distractions.

105

THE GOLDEN RULE

The golden rule of dog training is simple. For each 'question' (command), there is only one correct answer (reaction). One command = one reaction. Keep practising the command until the dog reacts correctly without hesitating. Be repetitive but not monotonous. Dogs get bored just as people do!

Keep increasing the length of your stroll until the dog will walk quietly beside you without pulling as long as you want him to heel. When you stop heeling, indicate to the dog that the exercise is over by verbally praising as you pet him and say 'OK, good dog.' The 'OK' is used as a release word meaning that the exercise is finished and the dog is free to relax.

If you are dealing with a dog who insists on pulling you around, simply 'put on your brakes' and stand your ground until the dog realises that the two of you are not going anywhere until he is beside you and moving at your pace, not his. It may take some time just standing there to convince the dog that you are the leader and you will be the one to decide on the direction and speed of your travel.

Each time the dog looks up at you or slows down to give a slack lead between the two of you, quietly praise him and say, 'Good heel. Good dog.' Eventually, the dog will begin to respond and within a few days he will be walking politely beside you without pulling on the lead. At first, the training sessions should be kept short and very positive; soon the dog will be able to walk nicely with you for increasingly longer distances. Remember also to give the dog free time and the opportunity to run and play when you have finished heel practice.

WEANING OFF FOOD IN TRAINING

Food is used in training new behaviours. Once the dog understands what behaviour goes with a specific command, it is time to start weaning him off the food treats. At first, give a treat after each exercise. Then, start to give a treat only after

TRAINING TIP

Play fetch games with your puppy in an enclosed area where he can retrieve his toy and bring it back to you. Always use a toy or object designated just for this purpose. Never use a shoe, stocking or other item he may later confuse with those in your wardrobe or underneath your chair.

every other exercise. Mix up the times when you offer a food reward and the times when you only offer praise so that the dog will never know when he is going to receive both food and praise and when he is going to receive only praise. This is called a variable ratio reward system and it proves successful because there is always the chance that the owner will produce a treat, so the dog never stops trying for that reward. No matter what, ALWAYS give verbal praise.

Once reliably trained, your Whippet should go into his crate voluntarily and will enjoy resting there. NEVER use the crate as a place of punishment.

OBEDIENCE CLASSES

It is a good idea to enrol in an obedience class if one is available in your area. If yours is a show dog, ringcraft classes would be more appropriate. Many areas have dog clubs that offer basic obedience training as well as preparatory classes for obedience competition. There are also local dog trainers who offer similar classes.

At obedience trials, dogs can earn titles at various levels of competition. The beginning levels of competition include basic behaviours such as sit, down, heel, etc. The more advanced levels of competition include jumping, retrieving, scent discrimination and signal work. The advanced levels require a dog and owner to put a lot of time and effort into their training and the titles that can be earned at these levels of competition are very prestigious.

Obedience work with Whippets tends to be more popular in the USA than in Britain, although there are staunch supporters throughout the world.

ACTIVITIES FOR THE WHIPPET

Whether a dog is trained in the structured environment of a

class or alone with his owner at home, there are many activities that can bring fun and rewards to both owner and dog once they have mastered basic control.

Teaching the dog to help out around the home, in the garden or on the farm provides great satisfaction to both dog and owner. In addition, the dog's help makes life a little easier for his owner and raises his stature as a valued companion to his family. It helps give the dog a purpose by occupying his mind and providing an outlet for his energy. There are also various

DID YOU KNOW?

If you want to be successful in training your dog, you have four rules to obey yourself:
1. Develop an understanding of how a dog thinks.
2. Do not blame the dog for lack of communication.
3. Define your dog's personality and act accordingly.
4. Have patience and be consistent.

The Whippet is an exceptionally intelligent dog, always willing to please. Be clear in indicating to your Whippet what you want him to do.

Training the Whippet for agility trials requires patience and experience. This Whippet is learning to 'weave.'

areas of the dog sport to consider if you are interested in participating in organised competition with your Whippet.

RACING, LURE COURSING AND COURSING

Track racing with Whippets is a sport well known, held in Britain under the auspices of the

Whippet Club Racing Association, but Whippets also successfully take part in lure coursing and in coursing proper.

In lure coursing, the dogs chase a lure, which of course cannot change direction, as can live quarry. Whippets cannot take part in lure coursing until they are a year old and can only run with others of the same breed. Taking place between spring and autumn, this is great fun and with less pressure than more competitive events.

Whippet coursing, which is where a dog chases a live hare, began in Britain in 1962. It was held under strict rules and in all weathers between the set dates of September 14 to March 11, inclusive. Enthusiasts used to join Whippet coursing clubs and travel up and down the country

DID YOU KNOW?

Occasionally, a dog and owner who have not attended formal classes have been able to earn entry-level

titles by obtaining competition rules and regulations from a local breed club and practising on their own to a degree of perfection. Obtaining the higher level titles, however, almost always requires extensive training under the tutelage of experienced instructors. In addition, the more difficult levels require more specialised equipment whereas the lower levels do not.

for their dogs to compete under a strict set of rules. Owners enjoyed this competitive sport thoroughly, but the Whippets seemed to enjoy it even more. Whippet coursing has been banned in the United Kingdom since 2005.

This is what a Whippet looks like when he is not interested in training; he refuses to make eye contact.

AGILITY
Several Whippets take part successfully in agility. Agility is a popular and exciting sport where dogs run through an

109

TRAINING TIP

Your dog is actually training you at the same time you are training him.

Dogs do things to get attention. They usually repeat whatever succeeds in getting your attention.

THERAPY WORK

The Whippet's delightful and loving personality makes the breed well suited to therapy work. The breed is clean, quiet and gentle and surely many people in homes, hospitals and hospices throughout the world derive great enjoyment and comfort from spending a little while with a Whippet therapy dog.

OBEDIENCE SCHOOL

A basic obedience beginner's class usually lasts for six to eight weeks. Dog and owner attend an hour-long lesson once a week and practise for a few minutes, several times a day, each day at home. If done properly, the whole procedure will result in a well-mannered dog and an owner who delights in living with a pet that is eager to please and enjoys doing things with his owner.

obstacle course that includes various jumps, tunnels and other exercises to test the dogs' speed and coordination. The owners run through the course beside their dogs to give commands and guide them through the exercises.

While competitive, agility is a thoroughly pleasant pastime for both dog and owner—though in agility plenty of stamina is required both by Whippet and owner!

First Aid at a Glance

Burns
Place the affected area under cool water; use ice if only a small area is burnt.

Bee/Insect bites
Apply ice to relieve swelling; antihistamine dosed properly.

Animal bites
Clean any bleeding area; apply pressure until bleeding subsides; go to the vet.

Antifreeze poisoning
Immediately induce vomiting by using hydrogen peroxide. Seek *immediate* veterinary care.

Fish hooks
Removal best handled by vet; hook must be cut in order to remove.

Abrasions
Clean the wound and wash out thoroughly with fresh water; apply antiseptic.

Car accident
Move dog from roadway with blanket; seek veterinary aid.

Shock
Calm the dog, keep him warm; seek immediate veterinary help.

Nosebleed
Apply cold compress to the nose; apply pressure to any visible abrasion.

Bleeding
Apply pressure above the area; treat wound by applying a cotton pack.

Heat stroke
Submerge dog in cold bath; cool down with fresh air and water; go to the vet.

Frostbite/Hypothermia
Warm the dog with a warm bath, electric blankets or hot water bottles.

 Remember: an injured dog may attempt to bite a helping hand from fear and confusion. Always muzzle the dog before trying to offer assistance.

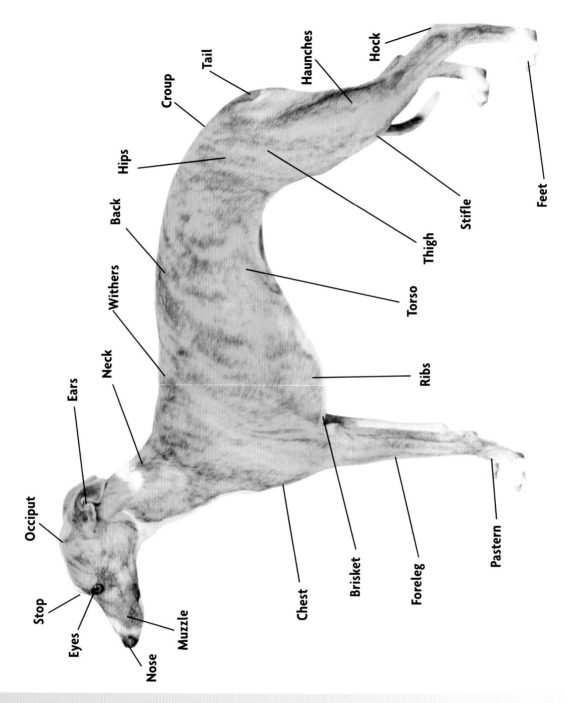

Physical Structure of the Whippet

WHIPPET

Dogs suffer many of the same physical illnesses as people. They might even share many of the same psychological problems. Since people usually know more about human diseases than canine maladies, many of the terms used in this chapter will be familiar but not necessarily those used by veterinary surgeons. We will use the term *x-ray*, instead of the more acceptable term *radiograph*. We will also use the familiar term *symptoms* even though dogs don't have symptoms, which are verbal descriptions of the patient's feelings: dogs have *clinical signs*. Since dogs can't speak, we have to look for clinical signs...but we still use the term *symptoms* in this book.

As a general rule, medicine is *practised*. That term is not arbitrary. Medicine is a constantly changing art as we learn more and more about genetics, electronic aids (like CAT scans) and daily laboratory advances. There are many dog maladies, like canine hip dysplasia, which are not universally treated in the same manner. Some veterinary surgeons opt for surgery more often than others do.

SELECTING A VETERINARY SURGEON

Your selection of a veterinary surgeon should not be based upon personality (as most are) but upon their convenience to your home. You require a veterinary surgeon who is close because you might have emergencies or need to make multiple visits for treatments. You require a vet who has services that you might require such as a tattooing and grooming facilities, as well as sophisticated pet supplies and a good reputation for ability and responsiveness. There is nothing more frustrating than having to wait a day or more to get a response from your veterinary surgeon.

All veterinary surgeons are

Before you buy a dog, meet and interview the veterinary surgeons in your area. Take everything into consideration; discuss background, specialities, fees, emergency policies, etc.

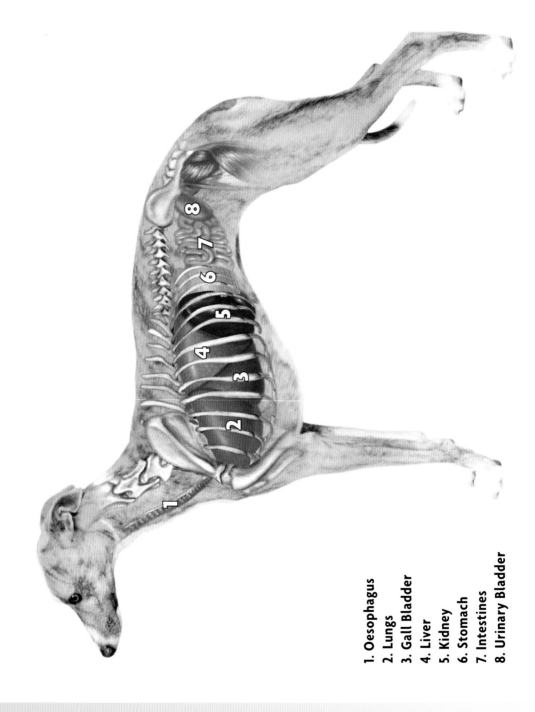

1. Oesophagus
2. Lungs
3. Gall Bladder
4. Liver
5. Kidney
6. Stomach
7. Intestines
8. Urinary Bladder

Internal Organs of the Whippet

licensed and their diplomas and/or certificates should be displayed in their waiting rooms. There are, however, many veterinary specialities that usually require further studies and internships. There are specialists in heart problems (veterinary cardiologists), skin problems (veterinary dermatologists), teeth and gum problems (veterinary dentists), eye problems (veterinary ophthalmologists), x-rays (veterinary radiologists), and surgeons who have specialities in bones, muscles or other organs. Most veterinary surgeons do routine surgery such as neutering and stitching up wounds. When the problem affecting your dog is serious, it is not unusual or

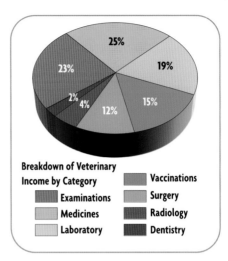

A typical American vet's income, categorised according to services provided. This survey dealt with small-animal practices.

Breakdown of Veterinary Income by Category

- Examinations
- Medicines
- Laboratory
- Vaccinations
- Surgery
- Radiology
- Dentistry

impudent to get another medical opinion, although in Britain you are obliged to advise the vets concerned about this. You might also want to compare costs amongst several veterinary surgeons. Sophisticated health care and veterinary services can be very costly. Don't be bashful about discussing these costs with your veterinary surgeon or his (her) staff. It is not infrequent that important decisions are based upon financial considerations.

PREVENTATIVE MEDICINE
It is much easier, less costly and more effective to practise preventative medicine than to fight bouts of illness and disease. Properly bred puppies come from parents that were selected based upon their genetic disease profile. Their mothers should have been vaccinated, free of all internal and

DID YOU KNOW?

Due to the Whippet's extreme low body fat, anaesthesia can be very dangerous for this breed, even for the

most routine procedures. Discuss this danger with your vet.

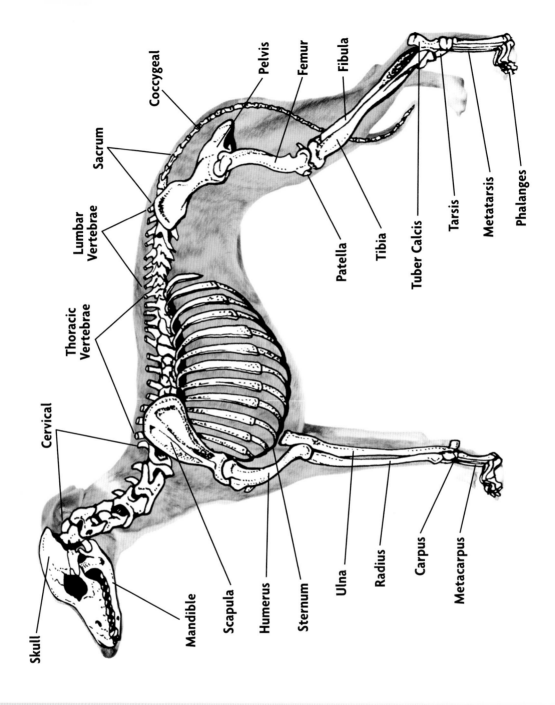

Skeletal Structure of the Whippet

external parasites, and properly nourished. For these reasons, a visit to the veterinary surgeon who cared for the dam (mother) is recommended. The dam can pass on disease resistance to her puppies, which can last for eight to ten weeks. She can also pass on parasites and many infections. That's why you should visit the veterinary surgeon who cared for the dam.

WEANING TO FIVE MONTHS OLD
Puppies should be weaned by the time they are about two months old. A puppy that remains for at least eight weeks with its mother and litter mates usually adapts better to other dogs and people later in its life.

Some new owners have their puppy examined by a veterinary surgeon immediately, which is a good idea. Vaccination programmes usually begin when the puppy is very young.

DID YOU KNOW?

Dogs who have been exposed to lawns sprayed with herbicides have double and triple the rate of malignant lymphoma. Town dogs are especially at risk, as they are exposed to tailored lawns and gardens. Dogs perspire and absorb through their footpads. Be careful where your dog walks and always avoid any area that appears yellowed from chemical overspray.

The puppy will have its teeth examined and have its skeletal conformation and general health checked prior to certification by the veterinary surgeon. Puppies in certain breeds have problems with their kneecaps, eye cataracts and other eye problems, heart murmurs and undescended testicles. They may also have personality problems and your veterinary surgeon might have training in temperament evaluation.

VACCINATION SCHEDULING
Most vaccinations are given by injection and should only be done by a veterinary surgeon. Both he and you should keep a record of the date of the injection, the identification of the vaccine and the amount given. Some vets give a first vaccination at eight weeks, but most dog breeders prefer the course not to commence until about ten weeks because of negating any antibodies passed on by the dam. The vaccination scheduling is usually based on a 15-day cycle. You must take your vet's advice as to when to vaccinate as this may differ according to the vaccine used. Most vaccinations immunise your puppy against viruses.

The usual vaccines contain immunising doses of several different viruses such as distemper, parvovirus, parainfluenza and hepatitis. There are

Normal hairs of a dog enlarged 200 times original size. The cuticle (outer covering) is clean and healthy. Unlike human hair that grows from the base, dog's hair also grows from the end, as shown in the inset. Scanning electron micrographs by Dr Dennis Kunkel, University of Hawaii.

other vaccines available when the puppy is at risk. You should rely upon professional advice. This is especially true for the booster-shot programme. Most vaccination programmes require a booster when the puppy is a year old and once a year thereafter. In some cases, circumstances may require more frequent immunisations. Kennel cough, more formally known as tracheobronchitis, is treated with a vaccine that is sprayed into the dog's nostrils. Kennel cough is usually included in routine vaccination, but this is often not so effective as for other major diseases.

FIVE MONTHS TO ONE YEAR
Unless you intend to breed or show your dog, neutering the puppy at six months of age is recommended. Discuss this with your veterinary surgeon.

By the time your Whippet is seven or eight months of age, he can be seriously evaluated for his

> ## 'P' STANDS FOR PROBLEM
>
> Urinary tract disease is a serious condition that requires immediate medical attention. Symptoms include urinating in inappropriate places or the need to urinate frequently in small amounts. Urinary tract disease is most effectively treated with antibiotics. To help promote good urinary tract health, owners must always be sure that a constant supply of fresh water is available to their pets.

> ## DID YOU KNOW?
>
> Cases of hyperactive adrenal glands (Cushing's disease) have been traced to the drinking of highly chlorinated water. Aerate or age your dog's drinking water before offering it.

conformation to the standard, thus determining show potential and desirability as a sire or dam. If the puppy is not top class and therefore is not a candidate for a serious breeding programme, most professionals advise neutering the puppy. Neutering has proven to be extremely beneficial to both male and female puppies. Besides eliminating the possibility of pregnancy, it inhibits (but does not prevent) breast cancer in bitches and prostate cancer in male dogs. Under no circumstances should a bitch be spayed prior to her first season.

Your veterinary surgeon should provide your puppy with a thorough dental evaluation at six months of age, ascertaining whether all the permanent teeth have erupted properly. A home dental care regimen should be initiated at six months, including brushing weekly and providing good dental devices (such as nylon bones). Regular dental care promotes healthy teeth, fresh breath and a longer life.

HEALTH AND VACCINATION SCHEDULE

Age in Weeks:	6th	8th	10th	12th	14th	16th	20-24th	1 yr
Worm Control	✔	✔	✔	✔	✔	✔	✔	
Neutering								✔
Heartworm		✔		✔		✔	✔	
Parvovirus	✔		✔		✔		✔	✔
Distemper		✔		✔		✔		✔
Hepatitis		✔		✔		✔		✔
Leptospirosis								✔
Parainfluenza	✔		✔		✔			✔
Dental Examination		✔					✔	✔
Complete Physical		✔					✔	✔
Coronavirus				✔			✔	✔
Kennel Cough	✔							
Hip Dysplasia								✔
Rabies*							✔	

Vaccinations are not instantly effective. It takes about two weeks for the dog's immunisation system to develop antibodies. Most vaccinations require annual booster shots. Your veterinary surgeon should guide you in this regard.
*Not applicable in the United Kingdom unless travelling abroad

ONE TO SEVEN YEARS

Once a year, your grown dog should visit the vet for an examination and vaccination boosters. Some vets recommend blood tests, thyroid level check and dental evaluation to accompany these annual visits. A thorough clinical evaluation by the vet can provide critical background information for your dog. Blood tests are often performed at one year of age, and dental examinations around the third or fourth birthday. In the long run, quality preventative care for your pet can save money, teeth and lives.

SKIN PROBLEMS IN WHIPPETS

Veterinary surgeons are consulted by dog owners for skin problems more than any other group of diseases or maladies. Dogs' skin is almost as sensitive as human skin and both suffer almost the same

DID YOU KNOW?

Your veterinary surgeon will probably recommend that your puppy be vaccinated before you take him outside. There are airborne diseases, parasite eggs in the grass and unexpected visits from other dogs that might be dangerous to your puppy's health.

ailments. (Though the occurrence of acne in dogs is rare!) For this reason, veterinary dermatology has developed into a speciality practised by many veterinary surgeons.

Since many skin problems have visual symptoms that are almost identical, it requires the skill of an experienced veterinary dermatologist to identify and cure many of the more severe skin disorders. Pet shops sell many treatments for skin problems but most of the treatments are directed at symptoms and not the underlying problem(s). If your dog

DID YOU KNOW?

Vaccines do not work all the time. Sometimes dogs are allergic to them and many times the antibodies, which are supposed to be stimulated by the vaccine, just are not produced. You should keep your dog in the veterinary clinic for an hour after it is vaccinated to be sure there are no allergic reactions.

DISEASE REFERENCE CHART

	What is it?	What causes it?	Symptoms
Leptospirosis	Severe disease that affects the internal organs; can be spread to people.	A bacterium, which is often carried by rodents, that enters through mucous membranes and spreads quickly throughout the body.	Range from fever, vomiting and loss of appetite in less severe cases to shock, irreversible kidney damage and possibly death in most severe cases.
Rabies	Potentially deadly virus that infects warm-blooded mammals. Not seen in United Kingdom.	Bite from a carrier of the virus, mainly wild animals.	1st stage: dog exhibits change in behaviour, fear. 2nd stage: dog's behaviour becomes more aggressive. 3rd stage: loss of coordination, trouble with bodily functions.
Parvovirus	Highly contagious virus, potentially deadly.	Ingestion of the virus, which is usually spread through the faeces of infected dogs.	Most common: severe diarrhoea. Also vomiting, fatigue, lack of appetite.
Kennel cough	Contagious respiratory infection.	Combination of types of bacteria and virus. Most common: *Bordetella bronchiseptica* bacteria and parainfluenza virus.	Chronic cough.
Distemper	Disease primarily affecting respiratory and nervous system.	Virus that is related to the human measles virus.	Mild symptoms such as fever, lack of appetite and mucous secretion progress to evidence of brain damage, 'hard pad.'
Hepatitis	Virus primarily affecting the liver.	Canine adenovirus type I (CAV-1). Enters system when dog breathes in particles.	Lesser symptoms include listlessness, diarrhoea, vomiting. More severe symptoms include 'blue-eye' (clumps of virus in eye).
Coronavirus	Virus resulting in digestive problems.	Virus is spread through infected dog's faeces.	Stomach upset evidenced by lack of appetite, vomiting, diarrhoea.

meaning that they carry, but are not affected by, the disease. These diseases pose serious problems to breeders because in some instances there is no method of identifying carriers. Often the secondary diseases associated with these skin conditions are even more debilitating than the skin disorder, including cancers and respiratory problems; others can be lethal.

Amongst the known hereditary skin disorders, for which the mode of inheritance is known, are acrodermatitis, cutaneous asthenia (Ehlers-Danlos syndrome), sabaceous adenitis, cyclic haematopoiesis, dermatomyositis, IgA deficiency, colour dilution alopecia, which is found in Whippets, and nodular dermatofibrosis. Some of these disorders are limited to one or two breeds and others affect a large number of breeds. All inherited diseases must be diagnosed and treated by a veterinary specialist.

As soft and cosy as the grass may be, fleas and ticks frequently infest these areas, waiting for the resting Whippet. Parasite bites are a common affliction during the summer months.

is suffering from a skin disorder, you should seek professional assistance as quickly as possible. As with all diseases, the earlier a problem is identified and treated, the more successful is the cure.

HEREDITARY SKIN DISORDERS
Veterinary dermatologists are currently researching a number of skin disorders that are believed to have a hereditary basis. These inherited diseases are transmitted by both parents, who appear (phenotypically) normal but have a recessive gene for the disease,

PARASITE BITES
Many of us are allergic to insect bites. The bites itch, erupt and may even become infected. Dogs have the same reaction to fleas, ticks and/or mites. When an insect lands on you, you have the chance to whisk it away with your hand. Unfortunately, when your dog is bitten by a flea, tick or mite, it can only scratch it away or bite it. By the time the

When grooming your Whippet, be on guard for abnormalities of the skin and coat.

dog has been bitten, the parasite has done some of its damage. It may also have laid eggs to cause further problems in the near future. The itching from parasite bites is probably due to the saliva injected into the site when the parasite sucks the dog's blood.

Auto-Immune Skin Conditions

Auto-immune skin conditions are commonly referred to as being allergic to yourself, whilst allergies are usually inflammatory reactions to an outside stimulus. Auto-immune diseases cause serious damage to the tissues that are involved.

The best known auto-immune disease is lupus, which affects people as well as dogs. The symptoms are variable and may affect the kidneys, bones, blood chemistry and skin. It can be fatal to both dogs and humans, though it is not thought to be transmissible. It is usually successfully treated with cortisone, prednisone or similar corticosteroid, but extensive use of these drugs can have harmful side effects.

Acral Lick Granuloma

Many dogs have a very poorly understood syndrome called acral lick granuloma. The manifestation of the problem is the dog's tireless attack at a specific area of the body, almost always the legs or paws. They

DID YOU KNOW?

It was announced in April 1999 that the severe quarantine laws imposed on animals entering Britain from other rabies-free countries would become a thing of the past by April 2001. Rather than being confined to a kennel for six months upon arrival in Britain, animals undergo a series of blood tests and vaccinations, and are identifed by microchip implantation. Qualified pets receive a 'health passport' that allows their owners to travel with them in between Britain and other (mostly European) countries.

Check with www.defra.gov.uk to see which countries are included in the PETS Passport Scheme. Although veterinary standards are high in some countries that are not included, recently infected dogs may test negative to the disease and, without the quarantine period, may unknowingly introduce rabies into previously unaffected countries.

lick so intensively that they remove the hair and skin leaving an ugly, large wound. Tiny protuberances, which are outgrowths of new capillaries, bead on the surface of the wound. Owners who notice their dogs' biting and chewing at their extremities should have the vet determine the cause. If lick granuloma is the cause, although there is no absolute cure, corticosteroids are the most common treatment.

AIRBORNE ALLERGIES

Another interesting allergy is pollen allergy. Humans have hay fever, rose fever and other fevers with which they suffer during the pollinating season. Many dogs suffer the same allergies. When the pollen count is high, your dog might suffer but don't expect him to sneeze and have a runny nose like a human would. Dogs react to pollen allergies the same way they react to fleas—they scratch and bite themselves.

Dogs, like humans, can be tested for allergens. Discuss the testing with your veterinary dermatologist.

FOOD PROBLEMS

FOOD ALLERGIES

Dogs are allergic to many foods that are best-sellers and highly recommended by breeders and veterinary surgeons. Changing the brand of food that you buy may not eliminate the problem if the element to which the dog is allergic is contained in the new brand.

Recognising a food allergy is difficult. Humans vomit or have rashes when they eat a food to which they are allergic. Dogs neither vomit nor (usually) develop a rash. They react in the same manner as they do to an airborne or flea allergy: they itch, scratch and bite. Thus making the diagnosis extremely difficult. Whilst pollen allergies and parasite bites are usually seasonal, food allergies are year-round

Information...

You are your dog's caretaker and his dentist. Vets warn that plaque and tartar buildup on the teeth will damage the gums and allow bacteria to enter the dog's bloodstream, causing serious damage to the animal's vital

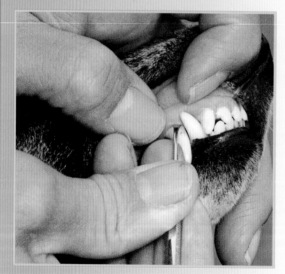

organs. Studies show that over 50 percent of dogs have some form of gum disease before age three. Daily or weekly tooth cleaning (with a brush or soft gauze pad wipes) can add years to your dog's life.

problems.

FOOD INTOLERANCE

Food intolerance is the inability of the dog to completely digest certain foods. Puppies that may have done very well on their mother's milk may not do well on cow's milk. The result of this food intolerance may be loose bowels, passing gas and stomach pains. These are the only obvious symptoms of food intolerance and that makes diagnosis difficult.

TREATING FOOD PROBLEMS

It is possible to handle food allergies and food intolerance yourself. Put your dog on a diet that it has never had. Obviously if it has never eaten this new food it can't have been allergic or intolerant of it. Start with a single ingredient that is not in the dog's diet at the present time. Ingredients like chopped beef or fish are common in dog's diets, so try something more exotic like rabbit, pheasant or even just vegetables. Keep the dog on this diet (with no additives) for a month. If the symptoms of food allergy or intolerance disappear, chances are your dog has a food allergy.

Don't think that the single ingredient cured the problem. You still must find a suitable diet and ascertain which ingredient in the old diet was objectionable. This is most easily done by adding ingredients to the new diet one at

Information...

Not every dog's ears are the same. Ears that are open to the air are healthier than ears with poor air circulation. Sometimes a dog can have two differ-

ently shaped ears. You should not probe inside your dog's ears. Only clean that which is accessible with a soft cotton wipe; do not use a cotton bud.

a time. Let the dog stay on the modified diet for a month before you add another ingredient. Eventually, you will determine the ingredient that caused the adverse reaction.

An alternative method is to carefully study the ingredients in the diet to which your dog is allergic or intolerant. Identify the main ingredient in this diet and eliminate the main ingredient by buying a different food that does not have that ingredient. Keep experimenting until the symptoms disappear after one month on the new diet.

A scanning electron micrograph (S. E. M.) of a dog flea, *Ctenocephalides canis.*

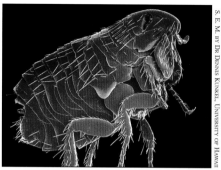

S. E. M. BY DR DENNIS KUNKEL, UNIVERSITY OF HAWAII

EXTERNAL PARASITES

Of all the problems to which dogs are prone, none is more well known and frustrating than fleas. Flea infestation is relatively simple to cure but difficult to prevent. Parasites that are harboured inside the body are a bit more difficult to eradicate but they are easier to control.

FLEAS

Magnified head of a dog flea, *Ctenocephalides canis.*

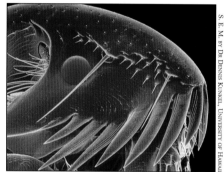

S. E. M. BY DR DENNIS KUNKEL, UNIVERSITY OF HAWAII

To control a flea infestation you have to understand the flea's life cycle. Fleas are often thought of as a summertime problem but centrally heated homes have changed the patterns and fleas can be found at any time of the year. The most effective method of flea control is a two-stage approach:

A male dog flea, *Ctenocephalides canis.*

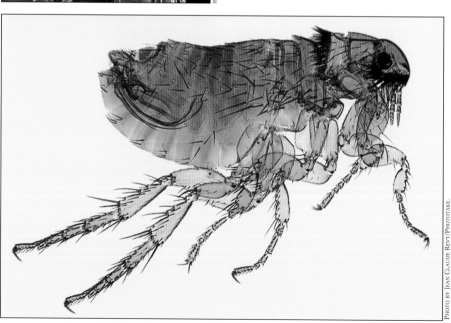

PHOTO BY JEAN CLAUDE REVY/PHOTOTAKE.

one stage to kill the adult fleas, and the other to control the development of pre-adult fleas. Unfortunately, no single active ingredient is effective against all stages of the life cycle.

LIFE CYCLE STAGES
During its life, a flea will pass through four life stages: egg, larva, pupa and adult. The adult stage is the most visible and irritating stage of the flea life cycle and this is why the majority of flea-control products concentrate on this stage. The fact is that adult fleas account for only 1% of the total flea population, and the other 99% exist in pre-adult stages, i.e. eggs, larvae and pupae. The pre-adult stages are barely visible to the naked eye.

THE LIFE CYCLE OF THE FLEA
Eggs are laid on the dog, usually in quantities of about 20 or 30, several times a day. The female adult flea must have a blood meal before each egg-laying session. When first laid, the eggs will cling to the dog's fur, as the eggs are still moist. However, they will quickly dry out and fall from the dog, especially if the dog moves around or scratches. Many eggs will fall off in the dog's favourite area or an area in which he spends a lot of time, such as his bed.

Once the eggs fall from the dog onto the carpet or furniture, they will hatch into larvae. This takes from one to ten days. Larvae are not particularly mobile, and will usually travel only a few inches from where they hatch.

A Look at Fleas

Fleas have been around for millions of years and have adapted to changing host animals. They are able to go through a complete life cycle in less than one month or they can extend their lives to almost two years by remaining as pupae or cocoons. They do not need blood or any other food for up to 20 months.

They have been measured as being able to jump 300,000 times and can jump 150 times their length in any direction including straight up. Those are just a few of the reasons why they are so successful in infesting a dog!

ILLUSTRATION COURTESY OF BAYER VITAL GMBH & CO. KG

However, they do have a tendency to move away from light and heavy traffic—under furniture and behind doors are common places to find high quantities of flea larvae.

The flea larvae feed on dead organic matter, including adult flea faeces, until they are ready to change into adult fleas. Fleas will usually remain as larvae for around seven days. After this period, the larvae will pupate into protective pupae. While inside the pupae, the larvae will undergo metamorphosis and change into adult fleas. This can take as little time as a few days, but the adult fleas can remain inside the pupae waiting to hatch for up to two years. The pupae are signalled to hatch by certain stimuli, such as physical pressure—the pupae's being stepped on, heat from an animal lying on the pupae or increased carbon dioxide levels and vibrations—indicating that a suitable host is available.

Once hatched, the adult flea must feed within a few days. Once the adult flea finds a host, it will

DID YOU KNOW?

Never mix flea control products without first consulting your veterinary surgeon. Some products can become toxic when combined with others and can cause serious or fatal consequences.

En Garde: CATCHING FLEAS OFF GUARD

Consider the following ways to arm yourself against fleas:
• Add a small amount of pennyroyal or eucalyptus oil to your dog's bath. These natural remedies repel fleas.
• Supplement your dog's food with fresh garlic (minced or grated) and a hearty amount of brewer's yeast, both of which ward off fleas.
• Use a flea comb on your dog daily. Submerge fleas in a cup of bleach to kill them quickly.
• Confine the dog to only a few rooms to limit the spread of fleas in the home.
• Vacuum daily...and get all of the crevices! Dispose of the bag every few days until the problem is under control.
• Wash your dog's bedding daily. Cover cushions where your dog sleeps with towels, and wash the towels often.

not leave voluntarily. It only becomes dislodged by grooming or the host animal's scratching. The adult flea will remain on the host for the duration of its life unless forcibly removed.

TREATING THE ENVIRONMENT AND THE DOG

Treating fleas should be a two-pronged attack. First, the environment needs to be treated; this includes carpets and furniture,

Opposite page: A scanning electron micrograph of a dog or cat flea, *Ctenocephalides*, magnified more than 100x. This image has been colourised for effect.

129

The Life Cycle of the Flea

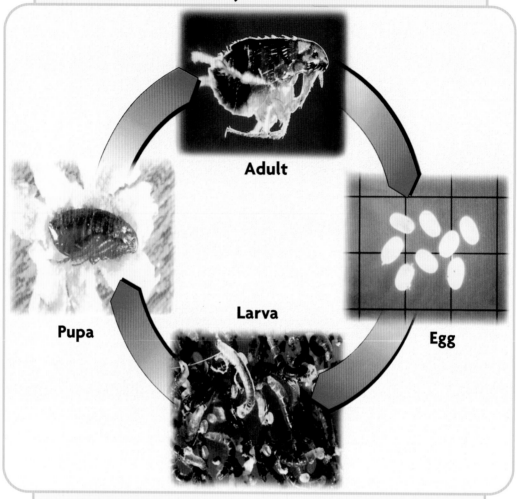

Adult

Pupa

Larva

Egg

This graphic depiction of the life cycle of the flea appears courtesy of Fleabusters®, Rₓ for fleas.

especially the dog's bedding and areas underneath furniture. The environment should be treated with a household spray containing an Insect Growth Regulator (IGR) and an insecticide to kill the adult fleas. Most IGRs are effective against eggs and larvae; they actually mimic the fleas' own hormones and stop the eggs and larvae from developing into adult fleas. There are currently no treatments available to attack the pupa stage of the life cycle, so the adult insecticide is used to kill the newly hatched adult fleas before they find a host. Most IGRs are active for many months, whilst

Photo by Dwight R Kuhn

the tropical and temperate world. They don't bite, like fleas; they harpoon. They dig their sharp proboscis (nose) into the dog's skin and drink the blood. Their only food and drink is dog's blood. Dogs can get Lyme disease, Rocky Mountain spotted fever (normally found in the USA only), paralysis and many other diseases from ticks and mites. They may

Dwight R Kuhn's magnificent action photo showing a flea jumping from a dog's back.

adult insecticides are only active for a few days.

When treating with a household spray, it is a good idea to vacuum before applying the product. This stimulates as many pupae as possible to hatch into adult fleas. The vacuum cleaner should also be treated with a flea treatment to prevent the eggs and larvae that have been hoovered into the vacuum bag from hatching.

The second stage of treatment is to apply an adult insecticide to the dog. Traditionally, this would be in the form of a collar or a spray, but more recent innovations include digestible insecticides that poison the fleas when they ingest the dog's blood. Alternatively, there are drops that, when placed on the back of the animal's neck, spread throughout the fur and skin to kill adult fleas.

TICKS AND MITES

Though not as common as fleas, ticks and mites are found all over

FLEA CONTROL

Two types of products should be used when treating fleas—a product to treat the pet and a product to treat the home. Adult fleas represent less than 1% of the flea population. The pre-adult fleas (eggs, larvae and pupae) represent more than 99% of the flea population and are found in the environment; it is in the case of pre-adult fleas that products containing an Insect Growth Regulator (IGR) should be used in the home.

IGRs are a new class of compounds used to prevent the development of insects. They do not kill the insect outright, but instead use the insect's biology against it to stop it from completing its growth. Products that contain methoprene are the world's first and leading IGRs. Used to control fleas and other insects, this type of IGR will stop flea larvae from developing and protect the house for up to seven months.

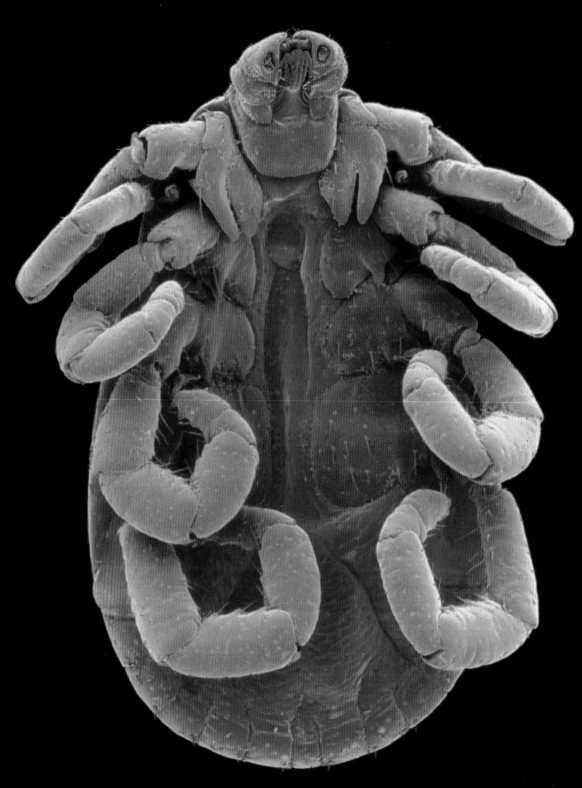

live where fleas are found and they like to hide in cracks or seams in walls wherever dogs live. They are controlled the same way fleas are controlled.

The dog tick, *Dermacentor variabilis*, may well be the most common dog tick in many geographical areas, especially those areas where the climate is hot and humid.

Most dog ticks have life expectancies of a week to six months, depending upon climatic conditions. They can neither jump

ILLUSTRATION COURTESY OF BAYER VITAL GMBH & CO. KG

Beware the Deer Tick

The great outdoors may be fun for your dog, but it also is a home to dangerous ticks. Deer ticks carry a bacterium known as *Borrelia burgdorferi* and are most active in the autumn and spring. When infections are caught early, penicillin and tetracycline are effective antibiotics, but if left untreated the bacteria may cause neurological, kidney and cardiac problems as well as long-term trouble with walking and painful joints.

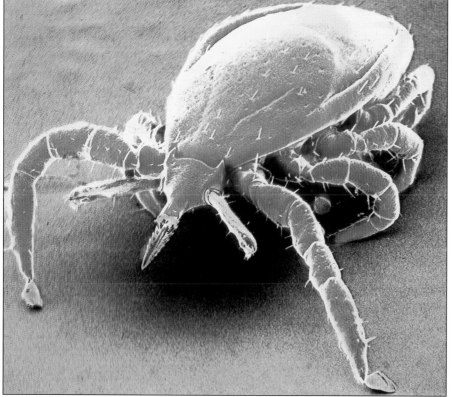

S. E. M. BY DR ANDREW SPIELMAN/PHOTOTAKE

A deer tick, the carrier of Lyme disease. This magnified micrograph has been colourised for effect.

Opposite page: The dog tick, *Dermacentor variabilis*, is probably the most common tick found on dogs. Look at the strength in its eight legs! No wonder it's hard to detach them.

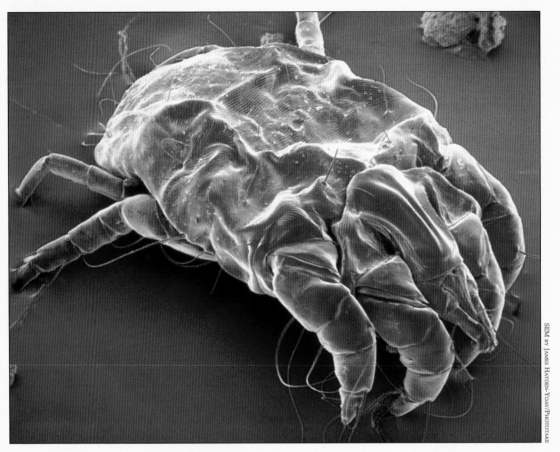

Above:
The mange mite,
Psoroptes bovis.

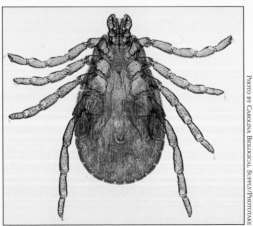

A brown dog tick, *Rhipicephalus sanguineus*, is
an uncommon but annoying tick found on dogs.

Human lice look like dog lice;
the two are closely related.

nor fly, but they can crawl slowly and can range up to 5 metres (16 feet) to reach a sleeping or unsuspecting dog.

MANGE

Mites cause a skin irritation called mange. Some are contagious, like *Cheyletiella*, ear mites, scabies and chiggers. Mites that cause ear-mite infestations are usually controlled with Lindane, which can only be administered by a vet, followed by Tresaderm at home.

It is essential that your dog be treated for mange as quickly as possible because some forms of mange are transmissible to people.

INTERNAL PARASITES

Most animals—fishes, birds and mammals, including dogs and humans—have worms and other parasites that live inside their bodies. According to Dr Herbert R Axelrod, the fish pathologist, there are two kinds of parasites: dumb and smart. The smart parasites live in peaceful cooperation with their hosts (symbiosis), while the dumb parasites kill their host. Most of the worm infections are relatively easy to control. If they are not controlled they weaken the host dog to the point that other medical problems occur, but they are not dumb parasites.

ROUNDWORMS

The roundworms that infect dogs are scientifically known as *Toxocara canis*. They live in the dog's intestine. The worms shed eggs continually. It has been estimated that a dog produces about 150 grammes of faeces every day. Each gramme of faeces averages 10,000–12,000 eggs of roundworms. There are no known areas in which dogs roam that do not contain roundworm eggs. The greatest danger of roundworms is that they infect people too! It is wise to have your dog tested regularly for roundworms.

DEWORMING

Ridding your puppy of worms is VERY IMPORTANT because certain worms that puppies carry, such as tapeworms and roundworms, can infect humans.

Breeders initiate a deworming programme at or about four weeks of age. The routine is repeated every two or three weeks until the puppy is three months old. The breeder from whom you obtained your puppy should provide you with the complete details of the deworming programme.

Your veterinary surgeon can prescribe and monitor the programme of deworming for you. The usual programme is treating the puppy every 15–20 days until the puppy is positively worm free.

It is not advised that you treat your puppy with drugs that are not recommended professionally.

ROUNDWORM

Average size dogs can pass 1,360,000 roundworm eggs every day.

For example, if there were only 1 million dogs in the world, the world would be saturated with 1,300 metric tonnes of dog faeces.

These faeces would contain 15,000,000,000 roundworm eggs.

It's known that 7–31% of home gardens and children's play boxes in the US contain roundworm eggs.

Flushing dog's faeces down the toilet is not a safe practice because the usual sewage treatments do not destroy roundworm eggs.

Infected puppies start shedding roundworm eggs at 3 weeks of age. They can be infected by their mother's milk.

Pigs also have roundworm infections that can be passed to humans and dogs. The typical roundworm parasite is called *Ascaris lumbricoides.*

HOOKWORMS

The worm *Ancylostoma caninum* is commonly called the dog hookworm. It is dangerous to humans and cats. It also has teeth by which it attaches itself to the intestines of the dog. It changes the site of its attachment about six times a day and the dog loses blood from each detachment, possibly causing iron-deficiency anaemia. Hookworms are easily purged from the dog with many medications. Milbemycin oxime, which also serves as a heartworm preventative in Collies, can be

The roundworm, *Rhabditis.* The roundworm can infect both dogs and humans.

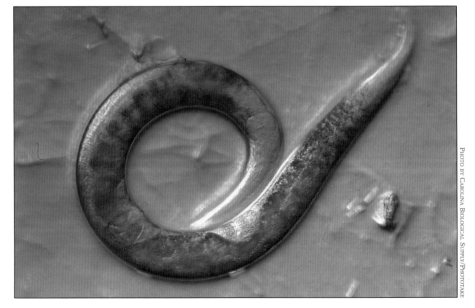

PHOTO BY CAROLINA BIOLOGICAL SUPPLY/PHOTOTAKE

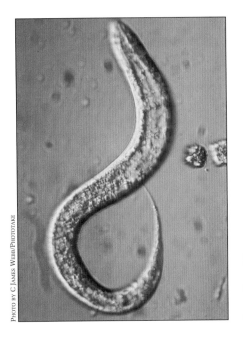

Photo by C James Webb/Phototake.

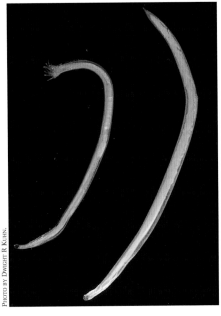

Photo by Dwight R Kuhn.

Left:
The infective stage of the hookworm larva.

Right:
Male and female hookworms, *Ancylostoma caninum*, are uncommonly found in pet or show dogs in Britain. Hookworms may infect other dogs that have exposure to grasslands.

used for this purpose.

In Britain the 'temperate climate' hookworm (*Uncinaria stenocephala*) is rarely found in pet or show dogs, but can occur in hunting packs, racing Greyhounds and sheepdogs because the worms can be prevalent wherever dogs are exercised regularly on grassland.

TAPEWORMS

There are many species of tapeworms. They are carried by fleas! The dog eats the flea and starts the tapeworm cycle. Humans can also be infected with tapeworms, so don't eat fleas! Fleas are so small that your dog could pass them onto your hands, your plate or your food and thus make it possible for you to ingest a flea which is carrying tapeworm eggs.

While tapeworm infection is not life threatening in dogs (smart parasite!), it can be the cause of a very serious liver disease for humans. About 50 percent of the

DID YOU KNOW?

Never allow your dog to swim in polluted water or public areas where water quality can be suspect. Even perfectly clear water can harbour parasites, many of which can cause serious to fatal illnesses in canines. Areas inhabited by waterfowl and other wildlife are especially dangerous.

The head and rostellum (the round prominence on the scolex) of a tapeworm, which infects dogs and humans.

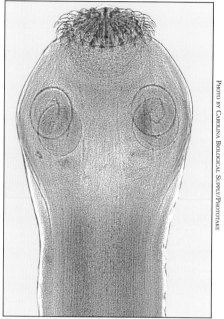

PHOTO BY CAROLINA BIOLOGICAL SUPPLY/PHOTOTAKE

humans infected with *Echinococcus multilocularis*, a type of tapeworm that causes alveolar hydatis, perish.

HEARTWORMS

Heartworms are thin, extended worms up to 30 cms (12 ins) long which live in a dog's heart and the major blood vessels surrounding it. Dogs may have up to 200 worms. Symptoms may be loss of energy, loss of appetite, coughing, the development of a pot belly and anaemia.

Heartworms are transmitted by mosquitoes. The mosquito drinks the blood of an infected dog and takes in larvae with the blood. The larvae, called microfilaria, develop within the body of the mosquito

TAPEWORM

Humans, rats, squirrels, foxes, coyotes, wolves, mixed breeds of dogs and purebred dogs are all susceptible to tapeworm infection. Except in humans, tapeworms are usually not a fatal infection.

Infected individuals can harbour a thousand parasitic worms.

Tapeworms have two sexes—male and female (many other worms have only one sex—male and female in the same worm).

If dogs eat infected rats or mice, they get the tapeworm disease.

One month after attaching to a dog's intestine, the worm starts shedding eggs. These eggs are infective immediately.

Infective eggs can live for a few months without a host animal.

Roundworms, whipworms and hookworms are just a few of the other commonly known worms that infect dogs.

and are passed on to the next dog bitten after the larvae mature. It takes two to three weeks for the larvae to develop to the infective stage within the body of the mosquito. Heartworms are rarely found in the UK but if you are travelling overseas with your dog there is risk of infection. Your vet will be able to advise you on preventative medicine before travelling.

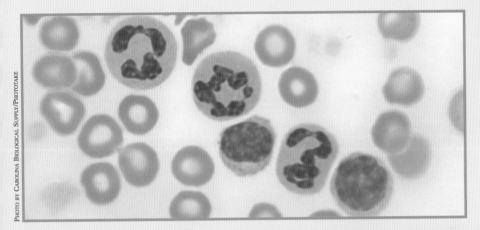

Magnified heartworm larvae, *Dirofilaria immitis*.

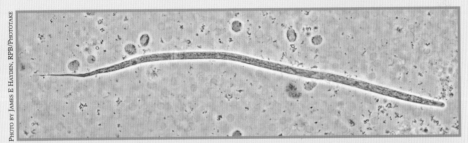

The heartworm, *Dirofilaria immitis*.

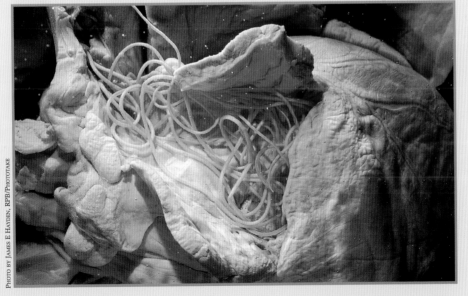

The heart of a dog infected with canine heartworm, *Dirofilaria immitis*.

139

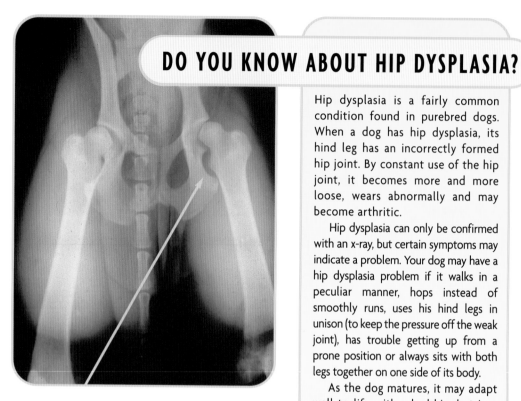

DO YOU KNOW ABOUT HIP DYSPLASIA?

Hip dysplasia is a fairly common condition found in purebred dogs. When a dog has hip dysplasia, its hind leg has an incorrectly formed hip joint. By constant use of the hip joint, it becomes more and more loose, wears abnormally and may become arthritic.

Hip dysplasia can only be confirmed with an x-ray, but certain symptoms may indicate a problem. Your dog may have a hip dysplasia problem if it walks in a peculiar manner, hops instead of smoothly runs, uses his hind legs in unison (to keep the pressure off the weak joint), has trouble getting up from a prone position or always sits with both legs together on one side of its body.

As the dog matures, it may adapt well to life with a bad hip, but in a few years the arthritis develops and many dogs with hip dysplasia become cripples.

Hip dysplasia is considered an inherited disease and can only be diagnosed definitively when the dog is two years old. Some experts claim that a special diet might help your puppy outgrow the bad hip, but the usual treatments are surgical. The removal of the pectineus muscle, the removal of the round part of the femur, reconstructing the pelvis and replacing the hip with an artificial one are all surgical interventions that are expensive, but they are usually very successful. Follow the advice of your veterinary surgeon.

Hip dysplasia is a badly worn hip joint caused by improper fit of the bone into the socket. It is easily the most common hip problem in larger dogs. The illustration shows a healthy hip joint on the left and an unhealthy hip joint on the right.

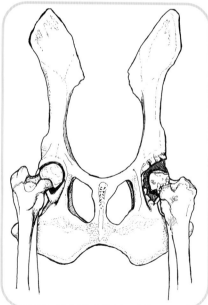

CDS
COGNITIVE DYSFUNCTION SYNDROME
'Old Dog Syndrome'

SYMPTOMS OF CDS

There are many ways to evaluate old-dog syndrome. Veterinary surgeons have defined CDS (cognitive dysfunction syndrome) as the gradual deterioration of cognitive abilities. These are indicated by changes in the dog's behaviour. When a dog changes its routine response, and maladies have been eliminated as the cause of these behavioural changes, then CDS is the usual diagnosis.

More than half the dogs over 8 years old suffer some form of CDS. The older the dog, the more chance it has of suffering from CDS. In humans, doctors often dismiss the CDS behavioural changes as part of 'winding down.'

There are four major signs of CDS: frequent toilet accidents inside the home, sleeps much more or much less than normal, acts confused, and fails to respond to social stimuli.

FREQUENT TOILET ACCIDENTS
- *Urinates in the house.*
- *Defecates in the house.*
- *Doesn't signal that he wants to go out.*

SLEEP PATTERNS
- *Moves much more slowly.*
- *Sleeps more than normal during the day.*
- *Sleeps less during the night.*

CONFUSION
- *Goes outside and just stands there.*
- *Appears confused with a faraway look in his eyes.*
- *Hides more often.*
- *Doesn't recognise friends.*
- *Doesn't come when called.*
- *Walks around listlessly and without a destination goal.*

FAILS TO RESPOND TO SOCIAL STIMULI
- *Comes to people less frequently, whether called or not.*
- *Doesn't tolerate petting for more than a short time.*
- *Doesn't come to the door when you return home from work.*

DID YOU KNOW?

The bottom line is simply that a dog is getting old when YOU think it is getting old because it slows down in its general activities, including walking, running, eating, jumping and retrieving. On the other hand, certain activities increase, such as more sleeping, more

barking and more repetition of habits like going to the door without being called when you put your coat on to leave or go outdoors.

The term *old* is a qualitative term. For dogs, as well as their masters, old is relative. Certainly we can all distinguish between a puppy Whippet and an adult Whippet—there are the obvious physical traits, such as size, appearance and facial expressions, and personality traits. Puppies that are nasty are very rare. Puppies and young dogs like to play with children. Children's natural exuberance is a good match for the seemingly endless energy of young dogs. They like to run, jump, chase and retrieve. When dogs grow up and cease their interaction with children, they are often thought of as being too old to play with the kids.

On the other hand, if a Whippet is only exposed to people over 60 years of age, its life will normally be less active and it will not seem to be getting old as its activity level slows down.

If people live to be 100 years old, dogs live to be 20 years old. Whilst this is a good rule of thumb, it is very inaccurate. When trying to compare dog years to human years, you cannot make a generalisation about all dogs. You can make the generalisation that 14 years is a good lifespan for a Whippet, which is quite good compared to many other purebred dogs that may only live to 8 or 9 years of age. Some Whippets have been known to live to 16 years. Dogs are generally considered mature within three years, but they can reproduce even earlier. So the first three years of a dog's life are like seven times that of comparable humans. That means a 3-year-old dog is like a 21-year-old human. As the curve of comparison shows, there is no hard and fast rule for comparing dog and human ages. The comparison is made even more difficult, for not all humans age

at the same rate...and human females live longer than human males.

WHAT TO LOOK FOR IN SENIORS

Most veterinary surgeons and behaviourists use the seventh year mark as the time to consider a dog a 'senior.' The term *senior* does not imply that the dog is geriatric and has begun to fail in mind and body. Ageing is essentially a slowing process. Humans readily admit that they feel a difference in their activity level from age 20 to 30, and then from 30 to 40, etc. By treating the seven-year-old dog as a senior, owners are able to implement certain therapeutic and preventative medical strategies with the help of their veteri-

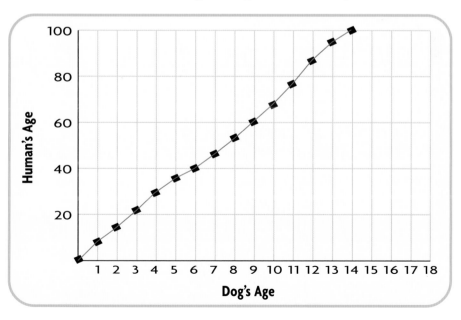

When Your Dog Gets Old...
Signs the Owner Can Look For

IF YOU NOTICE...	IT COULD INDICATE...
Discolouration of teeth and gums, foul breath, loss of appetite	Abcesses, gum disease, mouth lesions
Lumps, bumps, cysts, warts, fatty tumours	Cancers, benign or malignant
Cloudiness of eyes, apparent loss of sight	Cataracts, lenticular sclerosis, PRA, retinal dysplasia, blindness
Flaky coat, alopaecia (hair loss)	Hormonal problems, hypothyroidism
Obesity, appetite loss, excessive weight gain	Various problems
Household accidents, increased urination	Diabetes, kidney or bladder disease
Increased thirst	Kidney disease, diabetes mellitus
Change in sleeping habits, coughing	Heart disease
Difficulty moving	Arthritis, degenerative joint disease, spondylosis (degenerative spine disease)

If you notice any of these signs, an appointment should be made immediately with a veterinary surgeon for a thorough evaluation.

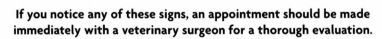

DID YOU KNOW?

Your senior dog may lose interest in eating, not because he's less hungry but because his senses of smell and taste have diminished. The old chow simply does not smell as good as it once did. Additionally, older dogs use less energy and thereby can sustain themselves on less food.

nary surgeons. A senior-care programme should include at least two veterinary visits per year, screening sessions to determine the dog's health status, as well as nutritional counselling. Veterinary surgeons determine the senior dog's health status through a blood smear for a complete blood count, serum chemistry profile with electrolytes, urinalysis, blood pressure check, electrocardiogram, ocular tonometry (pressure on the eyeball) and dental prophylaxis.

Such an extensive programme for senior dogs is well advised before owners start to see the obvious physical signs of ageing, such as slower and inhibited movement, greying, increased sleep/nap periods, and disinterest in play and other activity. This preventative programme promises a longer, healthier life for the ageing dog. Amongst the physical problems common in ageing dogs are the loss of sight and hearing, arthritis, kidney and liver failure, diabetes mellitus, heart disease and Cushing's disease (a hormonal disease).

BEHAVIOURAL CHANGES

Owners should avoid spoiling the older dog with too many fatty treats. Obesity is a common problem in older dogs and subtracts years from their lifespan. Keep the senior dog as trim as possible since excessive weight puts additional stress on the body's vital organs. Some breeders recommend supplementing the diet with foods high in fibre and lower in calories. Adding fresh vegetables and marrow broth to the senior's diet makes a tasty, low-calorie, low-fat supplement. Vets also offer speciality diets for senior dogs that are worth exploring.

In addition to the physical manifestations discussed, there are some behavioural changes and problems related to ageing dogs. Dogs suffering from hearing or vision loss, dental discomfort or arthritis can become aggressive. Likewise the near-deaf and/or blind dog may be startled more easily and react in an unexpectedly aggressive manner. Seniors suffering from senility can become more impatient and irritable. Housesoiling accidents are associated with loss of mobility, kidney problems, loss of sphincter control as well as plaque accumulation, physiological brain changes and reactions to medications.

Older dogs, just like young puppies, suffer from separation anxiety, which can lead to excessive barking, whining, housesoiling, and destructive behaviour. Seniors may become fearful of everyday sounds, such as vacuum cleaners, heaters, thunder, and passing traffic. Some dogs have difficulty sleeping, due

There are pet cemeteries located in towns and cities around the country. Consult your veterinary surgeon if you have difficulty in locating one.

to discomfort, the need for frequent potty visits and the like.

Your dog, as he nears his twilight years, needs his owner's patience and good care more than ever. Never punish an older dog for an accident or abnormal behaviour. For all the years of love, protection and companion-ship that your dog has provided, he deserves special attention and courtesies. The older dog may need to relieve himself at 3 a.m. because he can no longer hold it for eight hours. Older dogs may not be able to remain crated for more than two or three hours. It may be time to give up a sofa or chair to your old friend. Although he may not seem as enthusiastic about your attention and petting, he does appreciate the considera-tions you offer as he gets older.

Your Whippet does not understand why his world is slowing down. Owners must make the transition into the golden years as pleasant and rewarding as possible.

WHEN THE TIME COMES

You are never fully prepared to make a rational decision about putting your dog to sleep. It is very obvious that you love your Whippet or you would not be reading this book. Putting a loved dog to sleep is extremely difficult. It is a decision that must be made with your veterinary surgeon. You are usually forced to make the decision when one of the possible life-threatening symptoms becomes serious enough for you to seek medical (veterinary) help.

If the prognosis of the malady indicates the end is near and your beloved pet will only suffer more and experience no enjoyment for the balance of its life, then euthanasia is the right choice.

WHAT IS EUTHANASIA?

Euthanasia derives from the Greek meaning *good death*. In other words, it means the planned, painless killing of a dog suffering from a painful, incurable condition, or who is so aged that it cannot walk, see, eat or control its excretory functions.

Euthanasia is usually accomplished by injection with an overdose of an anaesthesia or barbiturate. Aside from the prick of the needle, the experience is usually painless.

MAKING THE DECISION

The decision to euthanise your dog is never easy. The days during which the dog becomes ill and the end occurs can be unusually stressful for you. If this is your first experience with the death of a loved one, you may need the comfort dictated by your religious beliefs. If you are the head of the family and have children, you should have involved them in the decision of putting your Whippet to sleep. Usually your dog can be maintained on drugs for a few days in order to give you ample time to make a decision. During this time, talking with members of your family or even people who have lived through this same experience can ease the burden of your inevitable decision.

THE FINAL RESTING PLACE
Dogs can have some of the same privileges as humans. They can occasionally be buried in their entirety in a pet cemetery, which is generally expensive, or if they have died at home can be buried in your garden in a place suitably marked with some stone or newly planted tree or bush. Alternatively they can be cremated and the ashes returned to you, or some people prefer to leave their dogs at the surgery for the vet to dispose of.

All of these options should be discussed frankly and openly with your veterinary surgeon. Do not be afraid to ask financial questions. Cremations can be individual, but a less expensive option is mass cremation, although of course the ashes can not then be returned.

GETTING ANOTHER DOG?
The grief of losing your beloved dog will be as lasting as the grief of losing a human friend or relative. In most cases, if your dog died of old age (if there is such a thing), it had slowed down considerably. Do you want a new Whippet puppy to replace it? Or are you better off finding a more mature Whippet, say two to three years of age, which will usually be house-trained and will have an already developed personality. In this case, you can find out if you like each other after a few hours of being together.

The decision is, of course, your own. Do you want another Whippet or perhaps a different breed so as to avoid comparison with your beloved friend? Most people usually buy the same breed because they know (and love) the characteristics of that breed. Then, too, they often know people who have the same breed and perhaps they are lucky enough that one of their friends expects a litter soon. What could be better?

WHIPPET

When you purchased your Whippet you will have made it clear to the breeder whether you wanted one just as a loveable companion and pet, or if you hoped to be buying a Whippet with show prospects. No reputable breeder will sell you a young puppy saying that it is *definitely* of show quality, for so much can go wrong during the early weeks and months of a puppy's development. If you plan to show, what you will hopefully have acquired is a puppy with 'show potential.'

To the novice, exhibiting a Whippet in the show ring may look easy but it takes a lot of hard work and devotion to do top winning at a show such as the prestigious Crufts, not to mention a little luck too!

The first concept that the canine novice learns when watching a dog show is that each breed first competes against members of its own breed. Once the judge has selected the best member of each breed, provided that the show is judged on a Group system, that chosen dog will compete with other dogs in its group. Finally the best of each

DID YOU KNOW?

You can get information about dog shows from kennel clubs and breed clubs:

Fédération Cynologique Internationale
14, rue Leopold II, B-6530 Thuin, Belgium
www.fci.be

The Kennel Club
1-5 Clarges St., Piccadilly
London W1Y 8AB, UK
www.thekennelclub.org.uk

American Kennel Club
5580 Centerview Drive
Raleigh, NC 27606-3390, USA
www.akc.org

Canadian Kennel Club
89 Skyway Ave., Suite 100
Etobicoke, Ontario
M9W 6R4 Canada
www.ckc.ca

group will compete for Best in Show and Reserve Best in Show.

The second concept that you must understand is that the dogs are not actually competing against one another. The judge compares each dog against the breed standard, which is a written description of the ideal specimen of the breed. Whilst some early breed standards were indeed based on specific dogs that were famous or popular, many dedicated enthusiasts say that a perfect specimen, described in the standard, has never been bred. Thus the 'perfect' dog never walked into a show ring, has never been bred and, to the woe of dog breeders around the globe, does not exist. Breeders attempt to get as close to this ideal as possible, with every litter, but theoretically the 'perfect' dog is so elusive that it is impossible. (And if the 'perfect' dog were born, breeders and judges would never agree that it was indeed 'perfect.')

If you are interested in exploring dog shows, your best bet is to join your local breed club. These clubs often host both Championship and Open Shows, and sometimes Match meetings and Special Events, all of which could be of interest, even if you are only an onlooker. Clubs also send out newsletters and some organise training days and seminars in order that people may learn more about their chosen breed. To locate the nearest breed club for you, contact The Kennel Club, the ruling body for the British dog world. The Kennel Club governs not only conformation shows but also working trials, obedience trials, agility trials and field trials. The Kennel Club furnishes the rules and regulations for all these events plus general dog registration and other

Showing your Whippet is both enjoyable and educational. Be a gracious winner or a supportive loser. Showing is about the dogs first!

basic requirements of dog ownership. Its annual show called the Crufts Dog Show, held in Birmingham, is the largest benched show in England. Every year around 20,000 of the UK's best dogs qualify to participate in this marvellous show which lasts four days.

The Kennel Club governs many different kinds of shows in Great Britain, Australia, South

Africa and beyond. At the most competitive and prestigious of these shows, the Championship Shows, a dog can earn Challenge Certificates, and thereby become a Show Champion or a Champion. A dog must earn three Challenge Certificates under three different judges to earn the prefix of 'Sh Ch' or 'Ch.' Note that some breeds must also qualify in a field trial in order to gain the title of full champion. Challenge Certificates are awarded to a very small percentage of the dogs competing, especially as dogs which are already Champions compete with others for these coveted CCs. The number of Challenge Certificates awarded in any one year is based upon the total number of dogs in each breed entered for competition. There are three types of Championship Shows, an all-breed General Championship show for all Kennel-Club-recognised breeds; a Group Championship Show, limited to breeds within one of the groups; and a Breed Show, usually confined to a single breed. The Kennel Club determines which breeds at which Championship Shows will have the opportunity to earn Challenge Certificates (or tickets). Serious exhibitors often will opt not to participate if the tickets are withheld at a particular show. This policy makes earning championships even more difficult to accomplish.

Open Shows are generally less competitive and are frequently used as 'practice shows' for young dogs. There are hundreds of Open Shows each year that can be invitingly social events and are great first show experiences for the novice. Even if you're considering just watching a show to wet your paws, an Open Show is a great choice.

Whilst Championship and Open Shows are most important for the beginner to understand, there are other types of shows in which the interested dog owner can participate. Training clubs sponsor Matches that can be entered on the day of the show for

CLASSES AT DOG SHOWS

There can be as many as 18 classes per sex for your breed. Check the show schedule carefully to make sure that you have entered your dog in the appropriate class. Among the classes offered can be: Beginners; Minor Puppy (ages 6 to 9 months); Puppy (ages 6 to 12 months); Junior (ages 6 to 18 months); Beginners (handler or dog never won first place) as well as the following, each of which is defined in the schedule: Maiden; Novice; Tyro; Debutant; Undergraduate; Graduate; Post-graduate; Minor Limit; Mid Limit; Limit; Open; Veteran; Stud Dog; Brood Bitch; Progeny; Brace and Team.

a nominal fee. In these introductory-level exhibitions, two dogs are pulled out of a hat and 'matched,' the winner of that match goes on to the next round, and eventually only one dog is left undefeated.

Exemption Shows are much more light-hearted affairs with usually only four pedigree classes and several 'fun' classes, all of which can be entered on the day of the show. The proceeds of an Exemption Show must be given to a charity. These shows are sometimes held in conjunction with small agricultural shows. Limited Shows are also available in small number, but entry is restricted to members of the club which hosts the show, although one can usually join the club when making an entry.

Before you actually step into the ring, you would be well advised to sit back and observe the judge's ring procedure. If it is your first time in the ring, do not be over-anxious and run to the front of the line. It is much better to stand back and study how the exhibitor in front of you is performing. The judge asks each handler to 'stand' the dog, hopefully showing the dog off to his best advantage. The judge will observe the dog from a distance and from different angles, approach the dog, check his teeth, overall structure, alertness and muscle tone, as well as consider

DOG SHOW ETIQUETTE

Just as with anything else, there is a certain etiquette to the show ring that can only be learned through experience. Showing your dog can be quite intimidating to you as a

novice when it seems as if everyone else knows what they are doing. You can familiarise yourself with ring procedure beforehand by taking a class to prepare you and your dog for conformation showing or by talking with an experienced handler. When you are in the ring, listen and pay attention to the judge and follow his/her directions. Remember, even the most skilled handlers had to start somewhere. Keep it up and you too will become a proficient handler before too long!

how well the dog 'conforms' to the standard. Most importantly, the judge will have the exhibitor move the dog around the ring in some pattern that he or she should specify (another advantage to not going first, but always listen since some judges change their directions, and the judge is always right!) Finally the judge will give the dog one last look before moving on to the next exhibitor.

If you are not in the top three at your first show, do not be discouraged. Be patient and consistent and you may eventually find yourself in the winning lineup. Remember that the winners were once in your shoes and have devoted many hours and much money to earn the placement. If you find that your dog is losing every time and never getting a nod, it may be time to consider a different dog sport or just enjoy your Whippet as a pet.

WORKING TRIALS
Working trials can be entered by any well-trained dog of any breed, not just Gundogs or Working dogs. Many dogs that earn the Kennel Club Good Citizen Dog award choose to participate in a working trial. There are five stakes at both open and championship levels: Companion Dog (CD), Utility Dog (UD), Working Dog (WD), Tracking Dog (TD) and Patrol Dog (PD). As in conformation shows, dogs compete against a standard and if the dog reaches the qualifying mark, it obtains a certificate. Divided into groups, each exercise must be achieved 70 percent in order to qualify. If the dog achieves 80 percent in the open

level, it receives a Certificate of Merit (COM), in the championship level, it receives a Qualifying Certificate. At the CD stake, dogs must participate in four groups: Control, Stay, Agility and Search (Retrieve and Nosework). At the next three levels, UD, WD and TD, there are only three groups: Control, Agility and Nosework.

Agility consists of three jumps: a vertical scale up a six-foot wall of planks; a clear jump over a basic three-foot hurdle with a removable top bar; and a long jump across angled planks stretching nine feet.

To earn the UD, WD and TD, dogs must track approximately one-half mile for articles laid from one-half hour to three hours ago. Tracks consist of turns and legs, and fresh ground is used for each participant.

The fifth stake, PD, involves teaching manwork, which is not recommended for every breed.

FIELD TRIALS AND WORKING TESTS
Working tests are frequently used to prepare dogs for field trials, the purpose of which is to heighten the instincts and natural abilities of Gundogs. Live game is not used in working tests. Unlike field trials, working tests do not count toward a dog's record at The Kennel Club, though the same judges often oversee

working tests. Field trials began in England in 1947 and are only moderately popular amongst dog folk. Whilst breeders of Working and Gundog breeds concern themselves with the field abilities of their dogs, there is considerably less interest in field trials than dog shows. In order for dogs to become full champions, certain breeds must qualify in the field as well. Upon gaining three CCs in the show ring, the dog is designated a Show Champion (Sh Ch). The title Champion (Ch) requires that the dog gain an award at a field trial, be a 'special qualifier' at a field trial or pass a 'special show dog qualifier' judged by a field trial judge on a shooting day.

AGILITY TRIALS

Agility trials began in the United Kingdom in 1977 and have since spread around the world, especially to the United States, where the sport enjoys strong popularity. The handler directs his dog over an obstacle course that includes jumps (such as those used in the working trials), as well as tyres, the dog walk, weave poles, pipe tunnels, collapsed tunnels, etc. The Kennel Club requires that dogs not be trained for agility until they are 15 months old. This dog sport intends to be great fun for dog and owner and interested owners should join a training

> ## FCI GROUPS
>
> FCI-recognised breeds are divided into ten groups:
> **Group 1:** Sheepdogs and Cattledogs (except Swiss Cattledogs)
> **Group 2:** Pinschers and Schnauzers, Molossians, Swiss Mountain Dogs and Swiss Cattledogs
> **Group 3:** Terriers
> **Group 4:** Dachshunds
> **Group 5:** Spitz- and primitive-type dogs
> **Group 6:** Scenthounds and related breeds
> **Group 7:** Pointing dogs
> **Group 8:** Retrievers, Flushing dogs and Water dogs
> **Group 9:** Companion and Toy dogs
> **Group 10:** Sighthounds

club that has obstacles and experienced agility handlers who can introduce you and your dog to the 'ropes' (and tyres, tunnels and so on).

FÉDÉRATION CYNOLOGIQUE INTERNATIONALE

Established in 1911, the Fédération Cynologique Internationale (FCI) represents the 'world kennel club.' This international body brings uniformity to the breeding, judging and showing of purebred dogs. Although the FCI originally included only five European nations: France, Holland, Austria, Germany and Belgium (which remains its headquarters), the organisation today embraces nations on six continents and recognises well over 300 breeds of purebred dog. There are three titles attainable through the FCI: the International Champion, which is the most prestigious; the International Beauty Champion, which is based on aptitude certificates in different countries; and the International Trial Champion, which is based on achievement in obedience trials in different countries. Exhibitors from around the world participate in these impressive FCI spectacles, the largest of which is the World Dog Show, hosted in a different country each year. FCI sponsors both national and international shows. The hosting country determines the judging system and breed standards are always based on the breed's country of origin.

The FCI is divided into ten groups. At the World Dog Show, the following classes are offered for each breed: Puppy Class (6–9 months), Youth Class (9–18 months), Open Class (15 months or older) and Champion Class. A dog can be awarded a classification of Excellent, Very Good, Good, Sufficient and Not Sufficient. Puppies can be awarded classifications of Very Promising, Promising or Not Promising. Four placements are made in each class. After all sexes and classes are judged, a Best of

Breed is selected. Other special groups and classes may also be shown. Each exhibitor showing a dog receives a written evaluation from the judge.

Besides the World Dog Show, you can exhibit your dog at speciality shows held by different breed clubs. Speciality shows may have their own regulations.

Dog shows can be an infectious family outing, especially for the multi-group family.

My Whippet

PUT YOUR PUPPY'S FIRST PICTURE HERE

Dog's Name _____

Date _____ Photographer _____